ACT

FLASH REVIEW

OTHER TITLES OF INTEREST FROM LEARNINGEXPRESS

501 Grammar and Writing Questions

501 Reading Comprehension Questions

Grammar Success in 20 Minutes a Day

Reading Comprehension Success in 20 Minutes a Day

Vocabulary and Spelling Success in 20 Minutes a Day

Write Better Essays in 20 Minutes a Day

Writing Skills Success in 20 Minutes a Day

ACT FLASH REVIEW

NEW YORK

Library of Congress Cataloging-in-Publication Data
ACT flash review.—1st ed.
p. cm.
ISBN-13: 978-1-57685-896-7
ISBN-10: 1-57685-896-0
1. ACT Assessment—Study guides. I. LearningExpress (Organization)
LB2353.48.A2913 2012
378.1'662—dc23
2011041990

Printed in the United States of America

9 8 7 6 5 4 3 2 1

First Edition

ISBN 978-1-57685-896-7

For more information or to place an order, contact LearningExpress at:
2 Rector Street
26th Floor
New York, NY 10006

Or visit us at:
www.learnatest.com

CONTENTS

INTRODUCTION

ACT Vocabulary Flash Review includes pronunciation guides, definitions, sample sentences, and synonyms for 600 of the most common words you might encounter on the ACT. Studying and learning these words will help you succeed on the English, Reading, and Science subject areas of the exam.

About the ACT

The ACT is a national college admissions examination. It is comprised of four subject area tests in English, Mathematics, Reading, and Science, and includes 215 multiple-choice items. The ACT Plus Writing includes an additional Writing Test.

Altogether, the test takes about three and a half hours to complete (or just over four hours for the ACT Plus Writing), including a short break. The actual testing time is 2 hours and 55 minutes (plus another half hour for the ACT Plus Writing).

See the official ACT website for detailed information about the test, including information about testing dates and registration: www.actstudent.org

Vocabulary on the ACT

The English, Reading, and Science Tests each include several reading passages. For this reason, the richer your vocabulary, the better you are likely to perform on the ACT. Only the Reading Test includes items that assess your comprehension of specific words, but none of these items tests your understanding of vocabulary out of context. This is good news for you! The context provided by the passage on which each item is based will help trigger your recollection of the meaning of the words you study in this book and elsewhere.

Vocabulary on the English Test

The English Test includes five prose passages and 75 multiple-choice items. Forty-five minutes are allotted to this test. This test

- assesses your understanding of usage and mechanics, including punctuation, grammar and usage, and sentence structure.

- assesses your rhetorical skills, including strategy, organization, and style.
- does not assess spelling, vocabulary, or your ability to recall rules of grammar.

Some items offer alternatives to underlined sections of the passage. You need to decide which choice makes the most sense in the passage. Other items simply pose a question about a part of the passage or the passage as a whole. You must decide which choice best answers the question posed.

Vocabulary study will especially help you with the items on the English Test that assess your rhetorical skills. Many of these items focus on effective word choice and ask you to select the wording or phrasing that is clearest, most appropriate given the overall tone of the passage, or most appropriate given the purpose or audience of the passage.

Vocabulary on the Reading Test

The Reading Test includes four passages and 40 multiple-choice items. Thirty-five minutes are allotted to this test. This test

- assesses your comprehension of information directly stated in a passage.
- assesses your ability to make inferences and draw conclusions from the statements in a passage.

The passages are similar in level and type to the texts encountered in first-year college courses. Items do not ask about information other than what is included in the passages, but rather focus on the main ideas, important details, the sequence of events, cause-and-effect relationships, voice, and strategies in each passage. Some of the items on the Reading Test assess your comprehension of specific words within the context of a passage.

Vocabulary study will help you with all of the items on this test. The better you understand the vocabulary used in a passage, the better you will be able to comprehend and interpret the ideas in the passage.

Vocabulary on the Science Test

The Science Test includes seven sets of scientific information, including passages, and 40 multiple-choice items. Thirty-five minutes are allotted to this test. The scientific information may be presented

- as data in a graph or table or other schematic form.
- in a research summary.
- as conflicting hypotheses or views on a topic.

Responding to items on this test requires no advanced knowledge, but rather a general understanding of biology, chemistry, physics, and Earth and space sciences. The emphasis is on scientific reasoning, such as critical thinking, making generalizations, drawing conclusions, and making predictions, rather than on the recollection of material from your science courses.

The 100 science vocabulary words included in this book represent core concepts in the life sciences, physical sciences, and Earth and space sciences. Practice with and mastery of these words will help you review the basics from your science courses and prepare you to comprehend the passages on the Science Test. Although the test does not directly assess your reading comprehension, the better you understand the vocabulary used in a passage, the better you will be able to comprehend the ideas in the passage and apply scientific reasoning to those ideas.

About This Book

The 600 words in this book are divided into two lists. The first list includes words you may encounter on the English and Reading Tests. The second list, including 100 words, represents core concepts in the life sciences, physical sciences, and Earth and space sciences. Each list is presented in alphabetical order.

Each page in this book includes three words: on one side, the words are provided along with a guide to their pronunciation; on the reverse side, definitions, sample sentences, and synonyms (in the first list) are provided for each word. The pages are designed in this way so that you can test yourself on the meaning of each word.

The pronunciation of each word is spelled out; no diacritical marks are used. Following is a key to the spellings used to represent some common sounds.

g	girl
j	jelly
k	kite, cat
s	sun, celery
z	zest, cheese
zh	reach, measure
th	teeth
th'	father, this
ng	sing
a	hat
ah	far, father
aw	raw
ey	cake, eight
e	bed, said
ee	feet, tease
i	wish
ahy	bike
u	cup
yoo	music

uh	pencil, taken [schwa]
o	mop, sock
oh	coat, rope
oy	noise, boy
ou	pour, or
ow	cow, mouse
oo	room

The definitions provided for the words are not comprehensive but rather focus your attention on the meanings that are the most common. Because the best way to learn a vocabulary word is to learn it in context, a sample sentence illustrating its use is provided for each word. In the first list, synonyms are provided to further clarify the meaning of each word.

Using This Book for Vocabulary Study

In truth, vocabulary acquisition is the work of a lifetime. Do not try to learn all 600 words in this book at once. The best approach is to study the words in sets of about 12 or 15 words (4 or 5 pages) each day. Following is a suggested program of study:

- Review the set of words in the morning. Say each word aloud. Try to think of your own sentences using the words.

- Write the words down on a sheet of paper, and keep the sheet with you, checking it throughout the day to familiarize yourself with the list.
- In the evening, quiz yourself on the meaning of the words. Use a pencil to write a check next to the words you define correctly; review the words you are unable to define along with the words you study the next day.
- Periodically quiz yourself on the words you have already studied to check that you have learned them.

A Last Word on Vocabulary Study: Read, Read, Read

Vocabulary is learned best when it is learned in context—that's why we've provided a sample sentence for each word in this book. The more frequently you encounter words in a variety of contexts, the better you will be able to remember them and even discern the nuances of their meaning. So, the best way to learn ACT vocabulary is to read, read, read!

As a high school student, you likely have substantial reading assignments in all or most of your subjects each week. As you read, pay attention to the vocabulary in each assignment. Take the time to note and look up the meaning of words you don't know. If you come across one of the words in this book, note the context in which it is used. You might even want to jot down the sentence on the card with the word in this book.

Additionally, reading nonfiction that is *not* assigned to you in school will help you expand both your vocabulary and your reading comprehension skills. You can read about whatever interests you most: biographies, newspapers, magazines such as *Sports Illustrated* or *Rolling Stone*—and note that science magazines that include articles intended for a general audience, such as *Discover* or *National Geographic Magazine,* can especially help you prepare for the Science Test. And, in whatever you read, pay attention to the vocabulary you encounter. Learn the words that are new to you, and note the use of words you have learned from this book.

Part I

ACT VOCABULARY

ABHOR
(uhb-HOR)

ABJURE
(ab-JOOR)

ABORTIVE
(uh-BOUR-tiv)

to regard with repugnance, to loathe

I don't mind vacuuming, washing dishes, or doing most things that keep a house tidy, but I ***abhor*** *cleaning the toilet.*

Synonyms: despise, detest, hate, scorn

• •

to formally reject, often under oath

Though he was accused of treason, he would not ***abjure*** *his writings.*

Synonyms: forswear, renounce

• •

unsuccessful

The entrepreneurs learned much from their first, ***abortive*** *attempt to launch a new product, and their next offering was wildly successful.*

Synonyms: fruitless, ineffective

A

ABRIDGE
(uh-BRIJ)

ABROGATE
(A-bruh-geyt)

ABSOLVE
(ab-ZOLV)

to make shorter; to reduce in length, scope, or power

*We had to **abridge** our visit when our host came down with a terrible illness.*

Synonyms: condense, compress; diminish

• •

to officially or formally abolish, to do away with

*After the tyrant seized power, one of his first acts was to **abrogate** the right to a fair trial, and it was not long before all of his most vocal opponents were imprisoned.*

Synonyms: annul, dissolve

• •

to free from guilt or blame; to free from obligation or responsibility

*Though she was **absolved** of the crime in court, to the end of her days, townspeople treated her as though she had actually committed the murder.*

Synonyms: exonerate, forgive; liberate, release

ABSTEMIOUS
(ab-STEE-mee-uhs)

ACCENTUATE
(ak-SEN-choo-eyt)

ACCOLADE
(A-kuh-LEYD)

restrained, especially with food and alcohol

*In general, she is **abstemious** with desserts and sweets, but she does like to indulge in chocolate on occasion.*

Synonyms: frugal, moderate, restrained, temperate

• •

to emphasize or intensify

*Because I believe that confident writers are likely to become good writers, I tend to **accentuate** the positive in responding to my students' papers.*

Synonyms: feature, highlight, stress, underscore

• •

an award or other expression of honor or praise

*The film received many **accolades**, including the Oscar for Best Picture.*

Synonyms: award, honor

ACME
(AK-mee)

ACRIMONIOUS
(a-kri-MOH-nee-uhs)

ACUMEN
(uh-KYOO-muhn or AK-yuh-muhn)

the highest point

This novel represents the ***acme*** *of his accomplishment; nothing that he wrote before or after was even half as good.*

Synonyms: peak, summit

• •

bitter or biting in feeling, speech, or behavior

They were once best friends, but after their falling out, they had only ***acrimonious*** *words for each other.*

Synonyms: caustic, sarcastic, trenchant

• •

insight or shrewdness, usually in practical matters

Perhaps if he had applied his financial ***acumen*** *in his personal affairs as well as he did in business, he would not have gone bankrupt.*

Synonyms: discernment, insight, judgment, perception

ADAPT
(uh-DAPT)

ADROIT
(uh-DROYT)

ADULATION
(a-juh-LEY-shun or *a-dyuh-LEY-shun)*

to make suitable for some purpose or situation

*At first, she disliked the new school, but she **adapted** quickly and soon made a lot of friends.*

Synonyms: acclimate, accommodate, adjust, conform

• •

skillful or resourceful in handling situations

*I wish I could be as **adroit** as she is in handling disputes between her students.*

Synonyms: clever, deft, dexterous, expert, masterful

• •

excessive admiration, praise, or devotion; flattery

*Despite the **adulation** of thousands upon thousands of fans, the pop star remained humble.*

Synonyms: devotion, fawning, flattery, worship

A

ADVERSITY
(ad-VUHR-suh-tee)

AESTHETIC
(es-THET-ik)

AFFABLE
(AF-uh-buhl)

a state of serious or ongoing difficulty

After they lost everything in the wildfire, they discovered that they were able to cope with ***adversity*** *very well.*

Synonyms: affliction, calamity, distress, misfortune

• •

having to do with beauty or the arts

One might wear such a boldly beautiful dress for its ***aesthetic*** *qualities, but certainly not for comfort.*

Synonym: artistic

• •

friendly and at ease with others

They could not have been any more different: She was ***affable*** *and had many friends, whereas he was shy and even sullen at times.*

Synonyms: amicable, gracious, pleasant, warm

AFFECTED
(uh-FEK-tid)

ALACRITY
(uh-LA-kri-tee)

ALLEVIATE
(uh-LEE-vee-eyt)

marked by an artificial manner

*Her accent is not **affected**; she was born in Poland and lived in London for many years.*

Synonyms: assuming, feigned, pretending, unnatural

• •

cheerful readiness

*Eager to meet their new baby, I replied to their invitation with **alacrity**.*

Synonyms: liveliness, promptness, willingness

• •

to lessen the burden, make easier

*Nothing but time can **alleviate** the pain of my migraines.*

Synonyms: allay, ease, lighten, relieve

A

ALLUSION
(uh-LOO-zhuhn)

AMELIORATE
(uh-MEEL-yuh-reyt or *uh-MEE-lee-uh-reyt)*

AMICABLE
(A-mi-kuh-buhl)

an indirect reference, often in literature

In T.S. Eliot's poem "The Waste Land," the opening line, "April is the cruelest month," is an ***allusion*** *to Geoffrey Chaucer's* The Canterbury Tales, *which opens with a celebration of the sweet showers and singing birds of April.*

Synonym: reference

• •

to get or make better

These new policies may ***ameliorate*** *the difficult situation, but they do not solve the fundamental problem.*

Synonyms: alleviate, improve, relieve

• •

characterized by friendliness and goodwill

Although they are divorced, their relationship is ***amicable****; in fact, I have never heard either of them say anything bad about the other.*

Synonyms: courteous, harmonious, peaceful, sociable

AMPLE
(AM-puhl)

ANACHRONISM
(an-NA-kruh-ni-zuhm)

ANALOGY
(a-NA-luh-jee)

enough or more than enough in size or capacity

*We had **ample** funds for our project and even had some money left over when it was complete.*

Synonyms: bountiful, extensive, large, plentiful

• •

a person or thing that is out of place in time

*The play was set during the American Revolution but was full of deliberate **anachronisms**, including television sets and machine guns.*

Synonym: misplacement

• •

a comparison between two things based on a similarity between them

*She believes that the common **analogy** between the brain and a computer fails to account for the complexity of the human mind.*

Synonyms: correspondence, likeness, similarity

A

ANIMOSITY
(an-uh-MO-suh-tee)

ANOMALY
(uh-NOM-uh-lee)

ANTAGONIST
(an-TA-guh-nist)

ill will or strong dislike that is typically expressed through action

*The **animosity** between the two teams often leads to bench-clearing brawls during games.*

Synonyms: antagonism, hostility

• •

something different, not regular

*The cancellation of our regular Tuesday morning meeting was an **anomaly**, but so was the two-foot snowfall.*

Synonyms: exception, irregularity, oddity

• •

one who works against, competes with, or opposes another

In Romeo and Juliet, *the Montague and Capulet families are **antagonists** until their enmity leads to the death of their children.*

Synonym: adversary

A

ANTEBELLUM
(an-ti-BEL-luhm)

ANTIDOTE
(AN-ti-doht)

ANTITHESIS
(an-TI-thuh-sis)

from before the time of a war, particularly the Civil War

*The **antebellum** South is often pictured as a place dominated by grandiose mansions and large plantations.*

• •

the remedy for a poison or disease; something that relieves, prevents, or acts against a problem

*She recovered soon after the doctor gave her the **antidote** to the venomous snakebite.*

Synonyms: cure, medicine

• •

contrast or opposition between two things or ideas; the direct opposite of

*Our trip turned out to be the **antithesis** of a vacation: The car broke down on our way there, the weather was terrible, and the office kept calling me.*

Synonyms: contradiction, converse

APATHY
(A-puh-thee)

APPEASE
(uh-PEEZ)

ARCANE
(ahr-KEYN)

lack of emotion or interest

*He accused the listless student of **apathy**.*

Synonyms: disregard, indifference

• •

to bring to a state of peace

*Giving your children sweets to keep them quiet may **appease** them now, but what might be the long-term effects of such bribery?*

Synonyms: calm, pacify, soothe

• •

known or understood only by a select few

*The meanings of Tarot cards are actually not so **arcane**; you can learn them in books you can get just about anywhere.*

Synonyms: esoteric, mysterious, obscure, secret

ARDENT
(AHR-dnt)

ARDUOUS
(AHR-joo-uhs)

ASCERTAIN
(as-er-TEYN)

full of passion or devotion

The candidate had a small group of ***ardent*** *supporters who were willing to do just about anything to keep her campaign going.*

Synonyms: eager, fervent, passionate, zealous

• •

extremely difficult; requiring much energy or effort

Running a marathon is hardly as ***arduous*** *as training to run a marathon is.*

Synonyms: exhausting, grueling, strenuous

• •

to find out for certain

In order to ***ascertain*** *the truth of your resume, our human resources department is likely to contact one or more of your former employers.*

Synonyms: confirm, determine, discover, establish

ASPIRE
(uh-SPAHY-uhr)

ASSUAGE
(uh-SWEYJ)

ASYMMETRICAL
(ey-suh-ME-tri-kuhl)

to desire or seek a particular accomplishment or attainment

*Whether as a movie star or as a rock star, he didn't care; he simply **aspired** to be a star.*

Synonyms: dream, pursue, strive

to decrease the intensity or severity of

*To **assuage** residents' fear of crime, building management makes sure that at least one security guard is present at all times.*

Synonyms: calm, ease, relieve

not symmetrical

*Because one of her eyes was blue and the other brown, her face looked more **asymmetrical** than most.*

Synonyms: awry, crooked, unbalanced

ATYPICAL
(ey-TIP-i-kuhl)

AUDACIOUS
(aw-DEY-shuhs)

AUSPICIOUS
(aw-SPI-shuhs)

not typical or usual

*His refusal to eat any breakfast was **atypical**, and his parents concluded that he was probably sick.*

Synonyms: abnormal, irregular, unusual

• •

daring, recklessly brave; inventive, unconventional

*The **audacious** child climbed to the top of the tallest oak in the yard.*

Synonyms: adventurous, bold, rash

• •

favorable, promising success; fortunate, prosperous

*Their beautiful wedding was an **auspicious** beginning to their marriage.*

Synonyms: opportune, promising

A

AUTOCRAT
(AW-tuh-krat)

AVARICE
(A-vuh-ris)

AVENGE
(uh-VENJ)

ACT VOCABULARY

a person who rules with unlimited authority and power

In his old age, he was more figurehead than ***autocrat*** *while his much younger wife controlled everything from behind the scenes.*

Synonyms: despot, tyrant

a greed for wealth that cannot be satisfied

It was not ***avarice*** *so much as insecurity that drove him to work so hard and accumulate so much wealth.*

Synonyms: covetousness, greed, rapacity

to take vengeance for or on behalf of another

In Shakespeare's play, Hamlet cannot decide whether or not to ***avenge*** *the death of his father by killing his uncle.*

Synonyms: punish, redress, vindicate

AVERSION
(a-VUHR-zhuhn)

AWE
(aw)

a desire to avoid or turn away from something in dislike; the cause or object of dislike

*His strong **aversion** toward snakes borders on a phobia.*

Synonyms: disgust, loathing, repugnance

• •

(*n.*) a feeling of dread, reverence, or wonder inspired by someone or something powerful, sacred, or sublime

*As we reached the summit, we gasped in **awe** at the gorgeous view of the valley below and the mountains beyond.*

Synonyms: admiration, amazement, veneration

(*v.*) to inspire with a feeling of awe

*The magician **awed** the children with a series of seemingly impossible tricks.*

Synonyms: amaze, astonish, daunt, intimidate

• •

BALK
(bawlk)

BAMBOOZLE
(bam-BOO-zuhl)

BANAL
(buh-NAL or *BEYN-l)*

to stop short as though encountering an obstacle and refuse to proceed; to put an obstacle in the way of

I was hoping to go on the trip, but I ***balked*** *when I saw the cost of airfare.*

Synonyms: hesitate; hinder, thwart

• •

to deceive through trickery; to confuse or frustrate

We were ***bamboozled*** *into paying twice as much as we would have paid if we had bought the tickets directly from the box office.*

Synonyms: hoodwink, swindle; perplex

• •

unoriginal, trite

The sentiments in these greeting cards are completely ***banal****; if you want to say something heartfelt and original, write it yourself.*

Synonyms: bland, conventional, hackneyed

BANTER
(BAN-tuhr)

• •

BELIE
(bih-LAHY)

• •

BELLICOSE
(BEL-i-kohs)

witty, joking conversation

Feeling far too tired to be all that clever myself, I could hardly keep up with the ***banter*** *at Allison's party last night.*

Synonyms: repartee, jest

• •

to reveal the falsehood of, contradict

She said that she was not frightened of the climb, but her trembling hands ***belied*** *her claim.*

Synonyms: disprove, negate, repudiate

• •

inclined or eager to fight

The ***bellicose*** *young man picked so many fights with his friends that they decided to stop hanging out with him.*

Synonyms: belligerent, combative, hostile, warlike

BENEFACTOR
(BE-nuh-fak-tuhr)

BENEVOLENT
(buh-NEV-uh-luhnt)

BERATE
(bi-REYT)

one who gives a benefit, such as a gift

*The **benefactor** who donated the funds for our new gymnasium has chosen to remain anonymous.*

Synonyms: contributor, philanthropist, sponsor, supporter

• •

tending to do good, characterized by goodwill

*Once our crotchety old neighbor realized that our intentions in visiting him were **benevolent**, he let us in and offered us some tea.*

Synonyms: altruistic, charitable, compassionate, kind, philanthropic

• •

to scold or condemn with energy and at length

*Do not **berate** the poor child for making such a common mistake!*

Synonyms: castigate, rebuke, reprimand, reproach

BESTOW
(be-STOH)

BEWILDER
(bi-WIL-duhr)

BIZARRE
(bi-ZAHR)

to give as a gift; to put to use

*We will **bestow** the prize on the author of the best poem.*

Synonyms: bequeath, confer, present; apply, devote

to confuse thoroughly

*This map **bewilders** me so much that I think we'll have better luck asking someone for directions.*

Synonyms: baffle, confound, fluster, perplex

outrageously strange or out of the ordinary

*His parents' **bizarre** behavior finally made sense to him when he realized that they were planning a surprise party for his birthday.*

Synonyms: eccentric, extraordinary, outlandish

BOISTEROUS
(BOY-ster-uhs)

BOMBASTIC
(bom-BAS-tik)

BOWDLERIZE
(BOHD-luh-rahyz)

noisy and rough, rowdy

*The elderly couple liked to sit at the playground because they enjoyed the **boisterous** energy of the children playing there.*

Synonyms: rambunctious, unrestrained

• •

obnoxiously pretentious in speech or writing

*It seemed as though the debaters thought that voters would prefer the candidate who was most **bombastic** rather than the one who was most persuasive.*

Synonym: pompous

• •

to modify (a book, for example) by taking out parts thought to be vulgar; to modify by abridging, simplifying, or otherwise changing the content or style

*The censors **bowdlerized** the script for the play such that the plot was unrecognizable, so the theatrical company decided to cancel the production.*

Synonyms: edit; censor

BOYCOTT
(BOY-kot)

BUFFOON
(buh-FOON)

BURLY
(BUHR-lee)

to refuse to buy, use, or deal with something, as a means of protest

*We plan to **boycott** that restaurant until the owner issues an apology to the family who was treated so poorly there last weekend.*

Synonyms: prohibit, reject

• •

a person who amuses others with jokes and silly behavior; a ridiculous or foolish person

*Kenneth acts like a **buffoon** whenever Jane is around, and I'm pretty sure it's because he doesn't know any other way to show that he likes her.*

Synonyms: clown, fool, joker

• •

having a strong and heavy build

*Being both **burly** and fleet on his feet, he was a talented football player.*

Synonyms: bulky, hefty, husky, stout

CACOPHONY
(kuh-KOF-uh-nee)

CADENCE
(KAY-dns)

CAJOLE
(kuh-JOHL)

a harsh, discordant sound

*The **cacophony** of screeching monkeys could be heard throughout the zoo.*

Synonyms: discord, noise

• •

the rhythmic flow or pattern of sound or motion

*The low tone of her voice and soothing **cadence** of her words soon lulled the children to sleep.*

Synonyms: beat, measure, pulse

• •

to persuade through flattery, promises, or gentle urging; to obtain through gentle persuasion

*We had to **cajole** the boys to come to the museum with us, but once they were there, they were glad they had come.*

Synonyms: coax, wheedle

CALAMITY
(kuh-LA-muh-tee)

CANNY
(KAN-ee)

CAPITULATE
(kuh-PI-chuh-leyt)

a terrible disaster, or misery caused by a disaster or misfortune

*The **calamity** was not so much the hurricane itself as the disorganized and inadequate response of the authorities.*

Synonyms: affliction, catastrophe, misfortune

• •

clever, shrewd

*A **canny** negotiator, he found a solution that pleased both parties.*

Synonyms: astute, ingenious, knowing, skilled

• •

to surrender, to give up resisting

*Although his troops were cornered and there was no way they could win the battle, the general refused to **capitulate**.*

Synonyms: concede, cede, defer, submit, yield

CAPRICIOUS
(kuhp-RI-shuhs or *kuhp-REE-shuhs)*

CAUSTIC
(KAWS-tik)

CENSORIOUS
(sen-SAWR-ee-uhs)

impulsive, tending to act according to whim

*The **capricious** toddler played with each toy for only a few minutes before pulling another one out of the bin.*

Synonyms: arbitrary, erratic, unpredictable

• •

able to burn or corrode; sarcastic

*Your criticism may have been accurate, but your **caustic** tone was unnecessary and hurt my feelings.*

Synonyms: acerbic, biting, harsh

• •

given to judgment or condemnation

*He was generally **censorious** with his students and so was neither popular nor particularly effective as a teacher.*

Synonyms: carping, critical, fault-finding

C

CESSATION
(se-SEY-shuhn)

CHARLATAN
(SHAR-luh-tuhn)

CHERUBIC
(che-ROO-bik)

a temporary or complete stopping

*Not until the **cessation** of the storm were we able to assess the damage.*

Synonyms: conclusion, termination

• •

one who pretends to have knowledge or ability, a quack or fraud

*He was exposed as nothing more than a **charlatan**, and his supposed medicines were found to be little more than sugar water.*

Synonyms: con, fake, phony

• •

like an angel or cherub, plump and sweetly innocent

*As babies, they were pudgy and **cherubic**; now, as toddlers, they are wild little hoodlums.*

Synonyms: adorable, childlike, cute

C

CHICANERY
(shi-KEEN-ree or *shi-KEE-nuh-ree)*

• •

CHIDE
(chahyd)

• •

CHIMERICAL
(kahy-MER-i-kuhl or *ki-MER-i-kuhl)*

deception through trickery

*His **chicanery** won him a fortune, but eventually the law caught up with him.*

Synonyms: artifice, cheating, subterfuge

• •

to scold, reproach, or harass

*The teacher **chided** the children for their tardiness.*

Synonyms: admonish, berate, reprimand, rebuke

• •

fantastic, imaginary

*da Vinci's **chimerical** drawings of flying machines are based on his observations of bat wings.*

Synonyms: fanciful, improbable, unrealistic, visionary

CHOLERIC
(KAW-luh-rik)

CHRONOLOGY
(kruh-NO-luh-jee)

CHURLISH
(CHUHR-lish)

easily angered, hot-tempered

*Her **choleric** temper mellowed as she grew older, and those who met her in her forties were surprised to learn that she had once been known for her tantrums.*

Synonyms: irascible, irritable, peevish

• •

the ordering of events in the sequence in which they occurred

*The historian devoted her research to reconstructing the **chronology** of the era in which this region was settled.*

Synonyms: record, history

• •

lacking civility, difficult to work with

*His **churlish** response to her simple request shocked and confused her, and she would have nothing to do with him afterward.*

Synonyms: rude, vulgar

CIRCUITOUS
(suhr-KYOO-i-tuhs)

CIRCUMLOCUTION
(suhr-kuhm-loh-KYOO-shuhn)

CIRCUMNAVIGATE
(suhr-kuhm-NA-vuh-geyt)

going in a winding, indirect way

*We took a **circuitous** route to get here, so the trip took much longer than we had expected.*

Synonyms: rambling, roundabout

• •

a roundabout or evasive way of speaking, the use of an excessively large number of words to express an idea

*His boss could always tell when he had made a mistake, because he was given to **circumlocution** whenever he felt guilty about something.*

Synonyms: euphemism, verbiage

• •

to travel around, especially by water

*Ferdinand Magellan led the first expedition to **circumnavigate** the globe, though he died in the Philippines and did not make it all the way around the earth himself.*

Synonym: circle

CLANDESTINE
(klan-DES-tin)

COALESCE
(koh-uh-LES)

COGENT
(KOH-juhnt)

conducted in secrecy, typically in order to subvert or deceive

*Their **clandestine** affair went on for nearly a decade, during which no one ever found out about their secret passion.*

Synonyms: concealed, stealthy, underground

• •

to come together into one body or whole

*As we brainstormed, our various ideas **coalesced** into a unified plan.*

Synonyms: combine, integrate

• •

very convincing and appealing to reason; relevant

*Her **cogent** reasoning in the debate won many supporters for her campaign.*

Synonyms: apt, compelling, persuasive, telling

COHERENT
(koh-HER-uhnt or koh-HEER-uhnt)

COLLABORATE
(kuh-LA-buh-reyt)

COLLOQUIAL
(kuh-LOH-kwee-uhl)

logically or aesthetically consistent or whole

*It took many drafts for me to write a **coherent** account of that difficult time in my life.*

Synonyms: harmonious, intelligible, organized

• •

to work together, cooperate

*The musicians admired each others' work and decided to **collaborate** on their next album.*

Synonyms: collude, cooperate

• •

having to do with ordinary conversation, familiar, informal

*One's **colloquial** language is generally more relaxed and sometimes more vivid than the language one uses in writing.*

Synonyms: everyday, vernacular

C

COMMEMORATE
(kuh-MEM-uh-reyt)

COMPLACENT
(kuhm-PLEY-suhnt)

COMPLICITY
(kuhm-PLIS-uh-tee)

to serve as a memorial of; to honor the memory of through a ceremony or other such observation

*Every year the students **commemorate** the founding of the school by laying a wreath on the founder's grave.*

Synonyms: celebrate, observe, remember, salute

• •

satisfied with one's own condition

*Eleanor became **complacent** after she earned high marks on several math tests, so she did not study for the next test.*

Synonyms: self-satisfied, smug, unconcerned

• •

association with or involvement in wrongdoing

*Though she had not stolen anything herself, her **complicity** in the crime included hiding some of the stolen goods in her home.*

Synonyms: collaboration, implication

COMPRESS
(kuhm-PRES)

CONCOMITANT
(kuhn-KO-mi-tuhnt)

CONCORD
(KON-kourd)

to press together; to make shorter or smaller

*One of his gifts as a poet included an ability to **compress** even a long story into just a few lines.*

Synonyms: consolidate; abbreviate, condense, shorten

accompanying

*She suffered both the turbulent boat ride and the **concomitant** nausea without complaining once.*

Synonyms: accessory, complementary, concurrent

a state of agreement between people, groups, or nations

*The general **concord** was disrupted when a developer proposed the building of a strip mall just within the town borders; as many townspeople passionately objected to the plan as approved of it.*

Synonyms: consensus, harmony

CONDONE
(kuhn-DOHN)

• •

CONFLAGRATION
(kon-fluh-GREY-shuhn)

• •

CONFORMIST
(kuhn-FOUR-mist)

to treat or regard something bad as acceptable or otherwise not a problem

*As a teacher, I certainly cannot **condone** any form of cheating.*

Synonyms: disregard, excuse, overlook

• •

a destructive fire; conflict or war

*Dozens of homes and much of the forest were lost in the **conflagration**.*

Synonyms: blaze, holocaust, inferno

• •

one who conforms, or acts in accord with the usual practices or standards of a given group

*His being a **conformist** was not based on any particular principles or beliefs; it simply had never occurred to him that he did not need to dress and behave just as everyone else did.*

Synonyms: follower

C

CONFOUND
(kuhn-FOWND)

CONGENIAL
(kuhn-JEE-nee-uhl or *kuhn-JEE-nyuhl)*

CONJECTURE
(kuhn-JEK-chr)

to confuse thoroughly

*The recipe **confounded** her so completely that she gave up on trying to make the fancy meal and ordered takeout instead.*

Synonyms: baffle, bewilder, frustrate, perplex

pleasant, agreeable; compatible, harmonious

*My coworkers are certainly **congenial** enough, but I rarely share much more with them than the usual pleasantries and a few smiles.*

Synonyms: delightful; cooperative, sympathetic

an inference or conclusion based on faulty evidence or guesswork; the formation of such an inference or conclusion

*Albert did very little research and based his paper mostly on **conjecture**.*

Synonyms: guess, presumption, supposition, surmise

CONSOLE
(kuhn-SOHL)

• •

CONSTRUE
(kuhn-STROO)

• •

CONUNDRUM
(kuh-NUHN-druhm)

to lessen the sorrow or trouble of

*There was nothing we could do to **console** the boy whose dog had died; only time would heal his grief.*

Synonyms: comfort, solace, soothe

• •

to interpret or explain the meaning or intention of

*Though you might **construe** my questioning as hostile, I assure you that I am not trying to assign blame but rather simply trying to uncover the truth.*

Synonyms: decipher, infer, translate

• •

a complicated problem; literally, a riddle with a pun or wordplay in its answer

*How they were going to get to three different appointments within two hours was a **conundrum** that they solved by canceling two of the appointments.*

Synonyms: puzzle, riddle, trick

C

CONVENTIONAL
(kuhn-VEN-shuh-nuhl)

CONVIVIAL
(kuhn-VI-vee-uhl)

COVERT
(KOH-vuhrt)

formed by agreement; ordinary or unoriginal, conforming with the standard or usual way of doing things

*Whereas the exterior of their home was **conventional** and easily blended into the suburban neighborhood, the interior was filled with the strange artwork that they had made and collected.*

Synonyms: commonplace, conservative, pedestrian

• •

enjoying company, food, and drink

*Helen is **convivial** and enjoys outings and parties, whereas her sister usually prefers to stay at home and read.*

Synonyms: agreeable, friendly, jovial

• •

hidden, secret

*The purpose of the **covert** operation was to incite a coup.*

Synonyms: concealed, covered, disguised

C

COVET
(KUHV-it)

COWER
(COW-uhr)

CREDULOUS
(KRE-djuh-luhs)

to crave wealth or possessions, often those belonging to another

*They all **coveted** the award, but unfortunately only one of them could win it.*

Synonym: desire

to shrink or crouch in fear or shame

*The children **cowered** in the shadows as the heavy footsteps approached.*

Synonyms: cringe, recoil, tremble

willing to believe

*Don't be so **credulous** about everything he tells you! He likes to make up stories.*

Synonyms: believing, gullible, unsuspecting

CULPABLE
(KUHL-puh-buhl)

• •

CURMUDGEON
(ker-MUH-juhn)

• •

deserving blame

*He clearly looked **culpable** of the crime; after all, the weapon was stashed in his room and had his fingerprints all over it.*

Synonyms: blameworthy, guilty, liable

• •

a bad-tempered person, usually an old man

*The old man had a reputation as a **curmudgeon**, and so trick-or-treaters avoided his house at Halloween.*

Synonyms: grouch, crank

• •

DEARTH
(duhrth)

DEBUNK
(dee-BUNGK)

DECIDUOUS
(di-SI-joo-wuhs)

a shortage, an inadequate supply

*The **dearth** of grocery stores in that neighborhood contributes to the poor health of its residents.*

Synonyms: deficiency, lack, scarcity

• •

to expose something as false

*She wrote the article to **debunk** the governor's claim that the change in policy would result in job losses.*

Synonym: expose

• •

having leaves that are shed annually

*In the autumn, the leaves of such **deciduous** trees as maples and elms turn brilliant colors before they fall.*

DECORUM
(di-KOUR-uhm or *di-KOHR-uhm)*

DEDUCTION
(di-DUHK-shuhn)

DEFINITIVE
(di-FI-nuh-tiv)

propriety and good taste

We took care to act with ***decorum*** *when we visited the senator's office to make our request.*

Synonyms: civility, convention, dignity

• •

the act of taking away or that which is taken away; the coming to a conclusion by reasoning, particularly from general premises, or a conclusion reached by such reasoning

Even though the salesperson offered a ***deduction*** *from the usual price, the car was still too expensive for us to buy.*

Synonyms: subtraction; conclusion

• •

authoritative, complete; providing a final solution

That's not the ***definitive*** *edition of the book; in fact, it's actually missing several chapters.*

Synonyms: conclusive, reliable

D

DEIGN
(deyn)

DELETERIOUS
(de-luh-TEER-ee-uhs)

DEMEANOR
(di-MEE-nuhr)

to condescend with reluctance

*As a high school senior, he would not **deign** to offer a ride to school to his neighbor, a mere freshman.*

Synonyms: consent, patronize, stoop

• •

harmful

*Though it is important to keep well hydrated during a marathon, drinking too much water during the race can be **deleterious** to the health—or even fatal.*

Synonyms: detrimental, hurtful, injurious, pernicious

• •

the way one bears oneself or behaves toward others

*Though his **demeanor** was formal and even a little intimidating, those who knew him well said that he was much warmer than his outward behavior seemed to indicate.*

Synonyms: attitude, bearing, conduct, manner

D

DENIGRATE
(DEN-i-greyt)

DENOUNCE
(di-NOWNS)

DEPLETE
(di-PLEET)

to attack the reputation or achievements of another

*They **denigrated** her fundraising project only because they were jealous of the admiration she was receiving from others for her generosity.*

Synonyms: belittle, criticize, disparage

• •

to condemn publicly; to accuse formally; to announce the termination of (a treaty or other agreement)

*We were told to **denounce** our former colleagues as traitors or face arrest ourselves.*

Synonyms: censure, criticize

• •

to lessen greatly or exhaust the quantity of

*She felt **depleted** of energy after the long training run.*

Synonyms: drain, exhaust, impoverish

D

DEPRAVITY
(di-PRA-vuh-tee)

• •

DERIDE
(di-RAHYD)

• •

DESECRATE
(DES-i-kreyt)

a state of corruption or evil; a corrupt act or practice

*He hurt himself through his **depravity** more than he did anyone else.*

Synonyms: contamination, degeneracy, degradation; vice

• •

to laugh at in scorn or ridicule

*His classmates **derided** him because of his stuttering.*

Synonyms: disparage, mock, scoff

• •

to disturb or harm the sanctity of, to treat irreverently

*Because of her decision to write about some unsavory episodes in the life of her subject, the biographer was accused of **desecrating** his memory.*

Synonyms: contaminate, pervert, profane

D

DESPAIRING
(di-SPAIR-ing)

DESPONDENT
(dih-SPON-duhnt)

DETER
(di-TUHR)

marked by despair, having no hope

*We didn't need to ask whether or not her team had won the game; her **despairing** look said everything.*

Synonyms: desperate, despondent, hopeless, pessimistic

• •

deeply discouraged

*After he failed to get the part in the play, he became **despondent** about his prospects as an actor.*

Synonyms: disconsolate, despairing, hopeless, dejected melancholy, miserable

• •

to discourage or prevent from acting or continuing

*No amount of rejection could **deter** her from writing and submitting her stories, until at last she had one published.*

Synonyms: dissuade, obstruct, prohibit

DETRIMENTAL
(de-truh-MEN-tl)

DIFFIDENT
(DIF-i-duhnt)

DILIGENT
(DIL-i-juhnt)

damaging, harmful

*By now, everyone should know that smoking is **detrimental** to one's health.*

Synonym: destructive

• •

hesitant, lacking in self-confidence

*However **diffident** she initially had been about her abilities on the soccer field, she overcame her uncertainty and eventually became a star player.*

Synonyms: shy, reserved, timid, unassertive, withdrawn

• •

characterized by steady effort

*Due to the **diligent** efforts of the staff, the job was done beautifully and delivered on time.*

Synonyms: attentive, conscientious, painstaking, persistent

DIMINUTIVE
(dih-MIN-yuh-tiv)

DISCREDIT
(dis-KRE-dit)

DISDAIN
(dis-DEYN)

extremely small

*Don't mistake her **diminutive** size as indicating any sort of weakness; though little, she is fierce.*

Synonyms: miniature, tiny

• •

to refuse to believe or cause others to disbelieve

*They used the most ridiculous tactics to **discredit** the candidate, but because of their persistence, he was easily defeated.*

Synonyms: doubt, question, reject

• •

(*n.*) contempt, scorn

*He considered them with **disdain** after they confessed to having cheated.*

Synonyms: arrogance, disregard

(*v.*) to look on with scorn; to refuse involvement with because of feelings of disdain for

*I **disdain** to watch any reality TV shows.*

Synonym: despise

D

DISPARAGE
(di-SPER-ij)

DIVERGE
(duh-VUHRJ or *dahy-VUHRJ)*

DIVULGE
(dahy-VUHLJ or *di-VUHLJ)*

to speak of slightingly; to lessen the reputation of

Perhaps it was harsh of me to ***disparage*** *your work, but it's clear that you put little effort into it.*

Synonyms: belittle, depreciate

• •

to go in different directions from a common point; to differ in character, form, or opinion; to change course

The roads ***diverge*** *about a mile from here; one goes north, and the other continues east.*

Synonyms: digress, separate; deviate

• •

to make a secret known

She told me that she had been on an interview for a different job and then asked me not to ***divulge*** *the information to anyone else.*

Synonyms: admit, disclose, tell

D

DUPLICITY

(doo-PLI-suh-tee)

deceit in speech or action, specifically by speaking or acting in contradictory ways with different people regarding the same situation or subject

*Her **duplicity** was discovered when the two compared notes and found that she had given different accounts of her actions to each.*

Synonyms: deception, fraud, trickery

EBB
(eb)

ECLECTIC
(e-KLEK-tik)

ECSTATIC
(ek-STA-tik)

(*n.*) the receding of a flood or the tide; a condition or point of decline

*With his career at a low **ebb**, he decided he had to take whatever job was offered to him.*

Synonyms: recession, withdrawal; deterioration

(*v.*) (of a flood or the tide) to recede; to decline or become worse

*As the tide **ebbs** from the shore, the children will collect shells left behind by the sea.*

Synonyms: abate, diminish

• •

choosing from a variety of sources; composed of a variety of styles, methods, or ideas

*Her taste in film was **eclectic**, including everything from old black-and-white romances to contemporary thrillers.*

Synonyms: assorted, diverse, varied

• •

marked by overwhelming happiness, rapture

*The family was **ecstatic** to learn that they had won the lottery.*

Synonyms: delirious, enthusiastic, overjoyed

E

EDIFY
(ED-uh-fahy)

EFFICACY
(EF-i-kuh-see)

EGREGIOUS
(ih-GREE-juhs)

ACT VOCABULARY

to instruct or enlighten, particularly in moral or spiritual matters

These medieval plays were intended to ***edify*** *the illiterate on biblical teachings.*

Synonyms: educate, improve

• •

the power to produce the desired effect

The ***efficacy*** *of the medication was such that the infection cleared within twenty-four hours.*

Synonyms: capability, competence, effectiveness

• •

extraordinarily or obviously bad

The latest edition of the book was ridden with ***egregious*** *errors, including, somehow, the misspelling of the author's name.*

Synonyms: flagrant, preposterous

ELEGY
(EL-i-jee)

ELICIT
(ih-LIS-it)

ELLIPSE
(ih-LIPS)

a poem or song expressing sorrow at the loss of one who has died

*The song was a moving **elegy** for those who lost their lives in the war.*

Synonyms: lament, requiem

• •

to draw or bring out

*The play **elicited** such powerful feelings that many people in the audience wept.*

Synonyms: evoke, obtain

• •

an oval-shaped conic section; the sums of the distances from each point on the curve of the ellipse to two focal points are equal

*Earth's orbit is in the shape of an **ellipse**, with the Sun at one of the two focal points.*

Synonym: oval

EMBARGO
(im-BAHR-goh)

EMINENT
(EM-uh-nuhnt)

EMPATHY
(EM-puh-thee)

an order of a government prohibiting commercial ships to leave or enter its ports; any legal restriction of trade or commerce

*The company lost millions of dollars during the **embargo** because it could not get its products to its customers abroad.*

Synonym: ban

• •

prominent, distinguished; noteworthy or otherwise obvious; jutting out or high

*We were awestruck to have such an **eminent** conductor agree to work with our small school orchestra.*

Synonyms: illustrious, prestigious; conspicuous

• •

identification with the feelings or thoughts of another; the imaginative projection of one's own feelings or thoughts onto an object

*She wept out of **empathy** for her friend's great loss.*

Synonyms: affinity, compassion

E

EMULATE
(EM-yuh-leyt)

ENCUMBER
(in-KUHM-buhr)

ENERVATE
(EN-er-veyt)

to try to equal or excel; to imitate

By the time he got to middle school, he had given up on trying to ***emulate*** *his older brother, an athlete, and instead turned his attention to the arts.*

Synonyms: compete, follow, rival

to weigh down, to hinder

Already ***encumbered*** *with debt, the couple faced further difficulties when he lost his job.*

Synonyms: burden, hamper, inconvenience, obstruct

to reduce the strength of

The illness ***enervated*** *him so much that he decided not to go on vacation with us; though he might enjoy the time at the lake, he feared that the trip there and back would require too much energy.*

Synonyms: debilitate, enfeeble, weaken

ENFRANCHISE
(in-FRAN-chahyz)

ENGENDER
(in-JEN-duhr)

ENIGMATIC
(en-ig-MA-tik)

to grant with the rights of a citizen, particularly the right to vote; to free from slavery

The 13th, 14th, and 15th Amendments to the Constitution ***enfranchised*** *African-American men by banning slavery, granting citizenship to all adult males, and granting them voting rights.*

Synonyms: emancipate, empower, liberate

• •

to bring into existence

Her capable handling of the crisis ***engendered*** *confidence in all of us.*

Synonyms: beget, generate, originate, produce

• •

puzzling, mysterious

Scholars and critics have written pages upon pages in various attempts to interpret the meaning of the ***enigmatic*** *last line of that poem.*

Synonyms: ambiguous, perplexing

E

ENNUI
(ahn-WEE)

EPHEMERAL
(ih-FEM-ruhl or *ih-FEM-uh-ruhl)*

EPIPHANY
(ih-PIF-uh-nee)

a feeling of weariness

*His **ennui** was apparent in his drooping eyelids and slow, slouching walk.*

Synonyms: boredom, dullness, languor

lasting a short time

*The cherry blossoms are **ephemeral**, often blooming and falling within a week.*

Synonyms: brief, fleeting, momentary, passing

a sudden perception of the essential meaning or nature of something; an appearance or manifestation of the divine

*While sitting in traffic one morning, he had an **epiphany** that led him to quit his job that very day so that he could focus his time and effort on his true desire to open his own restaurant.*

Synonyms: revelation, vision

EPOCH
(EE-pok)

EPONYMOUS
(eh-PON-uh-muhs)

EQUINOX
(EE-kwuh-noks)

a period of time characterized by distinctive events or developments; a distinctive event or period of time; an extended period of time

The Renaissance was an ***epoch*** *of cultural and intellectual transformation during which humanistic values flourished.*

Synonyms: age, era, time

• •

giving one's name to a group, place, work of art, and so on.

My good friend Charles is the ***eponymous*** *owner of Charlie's Diner downtown.*

• •

either of the two times of the year (in March, marking the beginning of spring, and in September, marking the beginning of autumn) when the sun crosses the plane of the earth's equator and night and day are of equal length all around the world

I especially look forward to the spring ***equinox****, because from that day until the day autumn begins, the days are longer than the nights.*

E

ERADICATE
(ih-RA-duh-keyt)

ERUDITE
(ER-oo-dahyt or *ER-yoo-dahyt)*

ESOTERIC
(es-uh-TER-ik)

to do away with completely

*Worldwide efforts are being made to **eradicate** polio.*

Synonyms: annihilate, eliminate, extinguish, obliterate, uproot

• •

learned

*The **erudite** young woman could read four different languages.*

Synonyms: educated, knowledgeable, studious

• •

known only by the initiated

*Though some of my ancestors were Gypsies, I know nothing about such **esoteric** arts as reading palms.*

Synonyms: arcane, hidden, occult

E

ETHEREAL
(ih-THEER-ee-uhl)

EUPHEMISM
(YOO-fuh-mi-zuhm)

EVANESCENT
(ev-uh-NES-uhnt)

light and airy; delicate or refined; heavenly

The children's story was about fairies who lived in an ***ethereal*** *kingdom made of dewdrops and morning light.*

Synonyms: insubstantial; exquisite; celestial, unearthly

• •

the use of a neutral or vague word or phrase to replace a word or phrase that might offend or seem harsh or unpleasant

"Correctional facility" is a ***euphemism*** *for "prison."*

Synonyms: circumlocution, delicacy, pretense

• •

like vapor, tending to fade or vanish

The ***evanescent*** *trace of her perfume lingered in the air for a moment before it, too, vanished as she did.*

Synonyms: fleeting, passing, temporary, transient

EVENHANDED
(ee-vuhn-HAN-did)

EXACERBATE
(ig-ZA-suhr-beyt)

EXEMPLARY
(ig-ZEM-pluh-ree)

fair, impartial

*The judge's **evenhanded** decision satisfied both parties.*

Synonyms: balanced, equitable, unbiased

• •

to make more severe, bitter, or violent

*Our attempt to apologize for the lapse only seemed to **exacerbate** her bitterness toward us.*

Synonyms: aggravate, intensify, provoke

• •

worthy of imitation; serving as a warning; serving as a model or example

*His approach to training was **exemplary**, and those on the team who followed his example saw their own performance improve considerably.*

Synonyms: commendable; characteristic, representative

E

EXPONENT
(ik-SPOH-nuhnt)

EXPOUND
(ik-SPOUND)

EXPURGATE
(EK-spuhr-geyt)

one that explains or interprets; one that is a representative or advocate of something; in mathematics, a symbol written above and to the right of an expression, indicating the number of times the expression is used as a factor

*As an art historian, she strived to be an **exponent** of outsider artists whose work was otherwise likely to be misunderstood or forgotten.*

Synonyms: champion, proponent, supporter

• •

to set forth or explain in detail

*The teacher often digressed from the main topic in order to **expound** upon her own opinions and theories about history.*

Synonyms: discourse, explicate

• •

to remove objectionable or offensive words or passages, to cleanse of that which is considered morally offensive

*Wishing to protect his legacy, his family published an **expurgated** edition of his journals.*

Synonyms: purify, purge

E

EXULT
(ig-ZUHLT)

to rejoice

*We **exulted** when, after months of hard work, our team won the prize.*

Synonyms: celebrate, glory, revel

•••••••••••••••••••••••••••••••

FACETIOUS
(fuh-SEE-shuhs)

FACILITY
(fuh-SIL-i-tee)

FALLACY
(FAL-uh-see)

not serious, inappropriately jokey

*The teacher's **facetious** tone led us to believe that she was not serious about the homework assignment.*

Synonyms: amusing, frivolous, humorous

• •

ease due to aptitude or skill; the quality of being performed with ease

*He found that he had a **facility** with language, and so he had studied Spanish, French, and even Chinese before he got to college.*

Synonyms: adroitness, competence, proficiency

• •

a deceptive or mistaken idea or belief

*The clever mathematical proof seemed to show that 2 = 1, but it was based on a **fallacy**.*

Synonyms: delusion, error, misconception

FASTIDIOUS
(fa-STI-dee-uhs)

FATUOUS
(FACH-oo-uhs)

FECKLESS
(FEK-lis)

having excessively high standards; characterized by meticulous or excessive care

There is no need to be so ***fastidious*** *about this job; a mistake or two will be forgiven as long as you are able to work at a decent pace.*

Synonyms: demanding, exacting, particular; painstaking

• •

foolish

His ***fatuous*** *remarks amused no one but himself, and he managed to insult just about every woman at the party.*

Synonyms: idiotic, mindless, ridiculous, silly

• •

weak, ineffective; irresponsible

After a few ***feckless*** *attempts to correct our error, we just gave up.*

Synonyms: incompetent, futile, worthless; indifferent, lazy

FEIGN
(feyn)

FIDUCIARY
(fuh-DOO-shee-er-ee)

FILIBUSTER
(FIL-uh-buhs-tuhr)

to fake or pretend

*She **feigned** illness so that she would miss school on the day of the test.*

Synonyms: counterfeit, dissemble, pretend

• •

(*n.*) one who holds property or power in trust for another

*A **fiduciary** must not place personal interests above his or her duty to the trust.*

Synonyms: guardian, trustee

(*adj.*) of or related to the holding of something in trust; of, related to, or based on trust or confidence; depending on public confidence for value or currency

*By offering a retirement plan to employees, an employer takes on **fiduciary** responsibilities in administering the plan.*

• •

the use of obstruction to prevent action, especially the passage of a law

*The **filibuster** went on for two days, and ultimately there was no vote on the bill.*

Synonyms: delay, hindrance, interference, opposition

F

FINICKY
(FIN-i-kee)

FLAUNT
(flont)

FLEDGLING
(FLEJ-ling)

extremely particular

*Whereas I have always been willing to eat just about anything, my little sister was a **finicky** eater and even went through a period of refusing all foods but applesauce and macaroni and cheese.*

Synonyms: fastidious, fussy, picky

• •

to display or show off; to treat with contempt

*It was inconsiderate of Jessica to **flaunt** her wealth by telling Sheila all about her lavish vacation; Sheila, after all, has just lost her job.*

Synonyms: advertise, brandish, broadcast, flourish

• •

a beginner; literally, a bird that has just acquired feathers

*I apprenticed with him as a **fledgling** cook, long before I became a chef and opened my own restaurant.*

Synonyms: novice, rookie

FLOURISH
(FLUHR-ish)

FORMIDABLE
(FOUR-mi-duh-buhl or *four-MID-uh-buhl)*

FRACTIOUS
(FRAK-shuhs)

(*v.*) to grow vigorously, thrive; to prosper; to make grand, sweeping gestures; to add embellishments to writing

He had been a mediocre student in middle school, but he ***flourished*** *in high school.*

Synonyms: increase, succeed

(*n.*) a grand, sweeping gesture; a florid passage of speech or writing; an embellishment in writing or printing

Feeling pleased with what she had written, she added some ***flourishes*** *to her signature.*

Synonyms: embellishment, adornment

• •

inspiring fear or awe

It was a ***formidable*** *task, but through teamwork, careful study, and hours of effort, at last we completed the project.*

Synonyms: impressive, intimidating, tremendous

• •

tending to be quarrelsome or troublesome

The ***fractious*** *young men were constantly getting into trouble with both their teachers and their peers.*

Synonyms: unruly, rebellious, wayward, wild

F

FRAUGHT
(frot)

FURTIVE
(FUHR-tiv)

full of or attended by; causing or showing anxiety or tension

*Our path was **fraught** with danger and even took us through enemy territory, but we passed unharmed.*

Synonyms: replete; charged, uneasy

done secretly or in an underhanded way

*His **furtive** manner led me to suspect that he had done something illicit.*

Synonyms: cunning, sly, stealthy

GARGOYLE
(GAHR-goil)

GAUCHE
(gohsh)

GERRYMANDER
(JER-ee-man-duhr)

a grotesque carving of an animal or human figure, often functioning as a spout projecting from a gutter from which rainwater is thrown clear of the building

Both charming and hideous, ***gargoyles*** *can be found perched on the sides of medieval churches throughout Europe.*

• •

lacking social graces or sensitivity

I still cringe to think how ***gauche*** *I was to have asked such an insensitive question.*

Synonyms: awkward, crude, maladroit, tactless, uncouth

• •

(*n.*) the dividing of a state, county, or other region into election districts in such a way as to give one political party an electoral advantage

(*v.*) to divide a state, county, or other region into election districts in such a way as to give one political party an electoral advantage

Gerrymandering *is responsible for the long, narrow shape of our election district.*

G

GLOSSY
(GLOS-ee)

GLUTTON
(GLUHT-n)

GOAD
(gohd)

having a lustrous or shiny surface; attractive in an artificially smooth and sophisticated way

*She sanded, refinished, and polished the old wooden chair until it was smooth and **glossy** again.*

Synonyms: brilliant, polished, sleek

• •

one who tends to eat and drink greedily; one who has a great appetite or capacity for something

*Don't mistake her for a **glutton**; she eats so much not out of greed, but because she is training for a triathlon.*

Synonym: gourmand

• •

(*n.*) a pointed or electrically charged rod used for driving cattle and other animals; something that pains like such a rod; something that encourages or prods

*Her sharp words were like a **goad**, and he quickly did exactly what she demanded.*

Synonyms: incentive, motivation

(*v.*) to incite or prod with a goad or as if with a goad

*Their taunting **goaded** him to action.*

Synonyms: encourage, stimulate

G

GOURMAND
(goor-MAHND)

GRANDIOSE
(GRAN-dee-ohs or *gran-dee-OHS)*

GREGARIOUS
(gri-GAIR-ee-uhs)

one who is interested in good food and drink

*As a **gourmand**, he can think of no place in the world he would rather be than Italy, where good food and drink are truly appreciated.*

Synonyms: glutton, gourmet

• •

characterized by exaggerated grandeur; impressive due to size or grandeur

*The wealthy family lived in a **grandiose** mansion that looked out of place among the more modest homes in the town.*

Synonyms: ostentatious, overblown, pompous; magnificent

• •

tending to like to the company of others

*The **gregarious** couple frequently threw parties at their home.*

Synonyms: convivial, outgoing, sociable, social

GRIMACE
(GRI-muhs)

GROTTO
(GROT-oh)

GUERRILLA
(guh-RIL-uh)

a contorted facial expression that shows disgust or pain

*With a **grimace**, he looked through the trash bag to see if the package had been discarded by mistake.*

Synonyms: frown, scowl

• •

a cave; an artificial structure resembling a cave

*We liked to hear the echoes of our shouting inside the limestone **grotto** by the shore, but we had to leave before high tide, when the cave would flood.*

Synonym: cave

• •

(n.) an irregular soldier who fights through such tactics as surprise raids and sabotage

*Their war for independence was largely fought—and won—by **guerrillas**.*

Synonym: commando

(adj.) having to do with guerrillas or their tactics

*They were able to overcome a much larger, more conventional army because it was in no way prepared to confront their **guerrilla** tactics.*

G

GUILE
(gahyl)

GURU
(GOO-roo)

cunning, deceit

*The spy used both flattery and **guile** to win the trust of his target.*

Synonyms: duplicity, fraud, treachery, trickery

a spiritual or intellectual teacher, guide, or leader; one who gives counsel or advice

*Hundreds flocked to hear the financial **guru** share his wisdom on personal savings and investments.*

Synonyms: expert, master, sage

HACKNEYED
(HAK-need)

HAPLESS
(HAP-lis)

HEDONISM
(HEE-duh-ni-zuhm)

lacking originality

Neither its fast-paced action nor its talented lead actors could make up for the movie's ***hackneyed*** *revenge plot.*

Synonyms: banal, cliché, stale, trite

without luck

My ***hapless*** *younger brother broke his leg on the same day he lost his job.*

Synonyms: unfortunate, unlucky

devotion to pleasure, the doctrine that pleasure is the greatest good

A life of ***hedonism*** *is often a life that does not last long, as those who indulge in pleasure often do so at the expense of their health.*

Synonyms: debauchery, indulgence

HEGEMONY
(hi-JEM-uh-nee or *HEJ-uh-moh-nee)*

• •

HERITAGE
(HER-uh-tij)

• •

HOMAGE
(OM-ij)

powerful influence or authority over others, particularly social, cultural, or economic domination over others

*The **hegemony** of American culture throughout the world is undeniable.*

Synonym: predominance

• •

something, such as property or a tradition, inherited from one's ancestors; something possessed by reason of birth

*One aspect of our national **heritage** is a faith in dreaming big and striving to realize those dreams.*

Synonyms: birthright, legacy

• •

reverence or an expression of reverence

*In **homage** to her mentor, she dedicated her first novel to him.*

Synonym: tribute

HOMOGENEOUS
(hoh-muh-JEE-nee-uhs or *hoh-muh-JEEN-yuhs)*

HONE
(hohn)

HUBRIS
(HYOO-bris)

being of the same kind throughout, uniform; of the same kind

*Having grown up in a small town with a more or less **homogeneous** population, she longed to get away to a college in a big, diverse city.*

Synonyms: consistent; alike

• •

to sharpen; to make more acute or to improve

*Even a prima ballerina spends hours each week simply **honing** her skills.*

Synonyms: polish, perfect

• •

excessive self-confidence or pride

*In her **hubris**, she attempted to run a marathon with no training, and she was injured in the twelfth mile.*

Synonyms: arrogance, pretension, vanity

H

HYPERBOLE
(hahy-PUR-buh-lee)

HYPOCRISY
(hi-POK-ruh-see)

ACT VOCABULARY

extravagant and intentional exaggeration

*He's given to **hyperbole**, so if he said that it had taken him days to complete the project, you can guess that he really had spent a few hours on it, at most.*

Synonyms: embellishment, hype, overstatement

• •

a pretense of being more virtuous or religious than one actually is; an instance of such pretending

*His expressions of outrage are usually motivated by **hypocrisy**, not true empathy, and he rarely—if ever—follows up on them with any action.*

Synonyms: deceit, deception

• •

ICONOCLAST
(ahy-KON-uh-klast)

ILLUSORY
(ih-LOO-suh-ree or *ih-LOO-zuh-ree)*

ILLUSTRIOUS
(ih-LUHS-tree-uhs)

one who attacks accepted beliefs or institutions; literally, one who destroys religious images

*When he posted his Ninety-Five Theses, Martin Luther became the first **iconoclast** of the Protestant Reformation.*

Synonyms: dissident, heretic, radical, rebel

creating an illusion, unreal

*The grand prize promised by the sweepstakes was **illusory**; no one ever won it.*

Synonyms: chimerical, deceptive, misleading

notable or highly distinguished; (to describe actions or works) glorious

*He won the Nobel Prize for his **illustrious** achievements in literature.*

Synonyms: famous, renowned; outstanding

IMBIBE
(im-BAHYB)

IMMUNE
(ih-MYOON)

IMPAIR
(im-PAIR)

to drink; to soak up; to take in

In Paris, I plan to ***imbibe*** *both fine wine and the best art.*

Synonyms: consume; absorb; assimilate

• •

protected from a disease; having to do with the production of antibodies or lymphocytes; exempt, protected from

The doctor recommended that I have a booster dose of the vaccine, because my blood work showed that I am no longer ***immune*** *to the measles.*

Synonyms: resistant, unaffected

• •

to make worse

The injury ***impaired*** *his ability to get around, so he was late to work every day until his leg healed.*

Synonyms: damage, undermine, weaken

I

IMPASSIVE
(im-PAS-iv)

IMPEACH
(im-PEECH)

IMPERIOUS
(im-PEER-ee-uhs)

not subject to pain, without feeling or emotion

*She remained **impassive**, her voice steady and her expression unchanging even as they insulted her to her face.*

Synonyms: apathetic, dispassionate, stoic, unmoved

to charge a public official before a tribunal of misconduct in office; to challenge the credibility of; to accuse

*Almost certain that the House of Representatives would vote to **impeach** him, the president chose instead to resign.*

Synonyms: challenge, discredit, reprimand

domineering, haughty, or overbearing; urgent

*The new principal spoke to students in an **imperious** manner, and they instantly disliked him for talking down to them.*

Synonyms: autocratic, commanding, dictatorial; imperative

IMPERTINENT
(im-PUHR-tuh-nuhnt or *im-PUHRT-nuhnt)*

IMPERTURBABLE
(im-puhr-TUHR-buh-buhl)

IMPERVIOUS
(im-PUHR-vee-uhs)

not keeping within the bounds of propriety or good taste, characterized by rudeness; not relevant

*Her **impertinent** question offended the teacher, and he bellowed that she should mind her manners and her own business.*

Synonyms: intrusive; inappropriate, unsuitable

incapable of being disturbed

*Our dog goes wild with excitement whenever we have visitors, whereas our cat is **imperturbable**, hardly looking up from his spot on the couch.*

Synonyms: calm, composed, immovable, unexcited

not allowing entrance, incapable of being harmed or disturbed

*She was almost completely **impervious** to pain, which led her to take risks few would dare to try.*

Synonyms: immune, resistant, unaffected

I

IMPETUOUS
(im-PECH-oo-uhs)

IMPLICIT
(im-PLIS-it)

IMPUGN
(im-PYOON)

passionately impulsive

*Their **impetuous** decision to marry after knowing each other for hardly a week was one they later regretted.*

Synonyms: impassionate, spontaneous, unexpected

• •

implied, existing as a potential within

*Though she never actually said that she hoped you would stay home and attend the state college, it was **implicit** in all the hints she dropped about the schools she thought you might choose.*

Synonyms: understood, latent

• •

to attack as false

*How dare you **impugn** my motives when you have been so ambiguous about your own!*

Synonyms: challenge, dispute, malign, question

IMPULSIVE
(im-PUL-siv)

IMPUTE
(im-PYOOT)

INANE
(ih-NEYN)

arising from a sudden inspiration; tending to act on sudden inspirations; having the power to impel

It's typical for a toddler to spontaneously change her focus or direction when playing; I would actually be concerned if she were not ***impulsive****.*

Synonyms: instinctive, spontaneous, unpredictable

• •

to attribute or give credit to; to falsely or unjustly blame

Very young children tend to ***impute*** *special powers to their parents, who, after all, certainly are capable of a lot more than the typical one-year-old.*

Synonyms: ascribe; accuse

• •

ridiculous, lacking substance or meaning

The pop star's voice and music are incomparably good, but his lyrics are ***inane****; he really ought to have someone else write them for him.*

Synonyms: pointless, silly

INCOGNITO
(in-kog-NEE-toh)

INCONTROVERTIBLE
(in-kon-truh-VUHR-tuh-buhl)

INCULCATE
(in-KUHL-keyt or *IN-kuhl-keyt)*

with one's identity hidden

*To avoid the paparazzi and gossip journalists, the two movie stars planned to travel separately and **incognito**.*

Synonyms: anonymous, concealed

• •

not open to question, indisputable

*Though each member of the executive team had a different plan in mind, it was **incontrovertible** that drastic action had to be taken if the company were not to fail.*

Synonyms: established, undeniable

• •

to instruct or implant through repetition or persistent teaching

*His constant quoting of tired old proverbs **inculcated** his grandchildren not with wisdom so much as with a loathing of proverbs.*

Synonyms: impart, impress, instill, program

I

INDOLENT
(IN-duh-luhnt)

INEFFABLE
(in-EF-uh-buhl)

INEFFICACIOUS
(in-ef-uh-KEY-shuhs)

lazy

*The **indolent** young man did nothing but watch TV all day.*

Synonyms: idle, inactive, slothful, sluggish

• •

not capable of being described or expressed; not to be spoken because of taboo

*Her joy was **ineffable**; she could hardly utter a thanks, but truly her smile said all.*

Synonyms: indescribable, inexpressible, transcendent; unutterable

• •

not producing the desired effect

*Their protests against the bill were **inefficacious**; the governor signed it into law that very afternoon.*

Synonyms: inadequate, incompetent, ineffective, unsuccessful

I

INEPT
(in-EPT)

INEVITABLE
(in-EV-i-tuh-buhl)

INEXORABLE
(in-EK-ser-uh-buhl)

ACT VOCABULARY

lacking in ability, skill, or sense

*However skillful the college football star was on the field, on the dance floor he was so **inept** that he kept stepping on his partner's feet.*

Synonyms: awkward, clumsy, incapable, incompetent

not to be avoided, certain to happen

*With so many of their best players injured, it was **inevitable** that the team would lose.*

Synonyms: inescapable, unavoidable

not to be affected or stopped, relentless

*Their progress across the field was **inexorable**, and the team easily scored another touchdown.*

Synonyms: inescapable, unalterable, unyielding

I

INFALLIBLE
(in-FAL-uh-buhl)

INFAMOUS
(IN-fuh-muhs)

INFERENCE
(IN-fer-uhns or IN-fruhns)

incapable of error; not likely to mislead or disappoint, trustworthy, certain

*She has an **infallible** memory and can recall details about events that occurred years ago.*

Synonyms: authoritative; sure, unfailing

• •

having a reputation for evil; causing ill repute

*His family was **infamous**, rumored to be responsible for much of the organized crime that plagued the city.*

Synonyms: disreputable; disgraceful, scandalous

• •

the act or process of inferring, or concluding from reasoning, premises, or evidence; that which is inferred

*I had to act before I knew all the facts, and so I made an **inference** based on both my observations of the situation and past experience.*

Synonyms: conclusion, interpretation

INFRASTRUCTURE
(IN-fruh-struhk-chuhr)

• •

INSIPID
(in-SIP-id)

• •

INSOLENT
(IN-suh-lunt)

the basic, underlying structure of a system or organization; the system of public works serving a region, municipality, or nation

*If we fail to invest in our **infrastructure**—including everything from bridges to schools—the economy is bound to suffer.*

Synonym: framework

• •

lacking taste, dull

*I would enjoy visiting him a lot more if he didn't play that **insipid** music all day long.*

Synonyms: banal, inane, vapid

• •

speaking or behaving with contempt

*Anna did very well on her schoolwork, but because of her arrogance and **insolent** behavior, none of her teachers liked her.*

Synonyms: contemptuous, disdainful, disrespectful, insulting, rude

INSULAR
(IN-suh-ler or *IN-syoo-luhr)*

INTER
(in-TUHR)

INTERLOCUTOR
(in-tuhr-LO-kyuh-tuhr)

isolated; narrow-minded; literally: having to do with an island or islands

*Their **insular** attitude toward outsiders is understandable given how little they have seen of people who did not grow up here.*

Synonyms: bigoted, parochial, provincial

• •

to place a dead body in a grave or tomb

*The body had been **interred** in a shallow grave in the woods.*

Synonyms: bury, entomb

• •

one who participates in a conversation or dialogue; one who questions another

*I could hear Daniel speaking to somebody in our front yard, but I could not identify his **interlocutor**.*

Synonyms: conversationalist; interrogator, interviewer

INTERNECINE
(in-ter-NES-een)

INTERPOLATE
(in-TUHR-puh-leyt)

INTERREGNUM
(in-tuhr-REG-nuhm)

of or involving mutually destructive conflict within a group

*The holidays are always unpleasant, due to the seemingly ancient **internecine** conflicts between the various members of my family, which get dredged up every year.*

Synonyms: domestic, internal

to add words into a conversation or text

*As he read the story to the class, the teacher couldn't help but **interpolate** with a commentary on the style of the writing.*

Synonyms: inject, insert, interject

the period between two regimes, when the throne is vacant; a period during which normal governmental authority is suspended; a pause or interruption in a series

*The eleven-year-long period between the execution of Charles I and the restoration of Charles II in England is known as the **Interregnum**.*

Synonyms: breach, break, interruption, interim

I

INTREPID
(in-TREP-id)

INTRICATE
(IN-tri-kit)

INTROSPECTION
(in-truh-SPEK-shuhn)

courageous

*Tenzing Norgay and Sir Edmund Hillary were the **intrepid** men who were the first to reach the summit of Mount Everest.*

Synonyms: bold, brave, fearless

having many interrelated parts or elements; difficult to understand, use, or make

*Her explanation of how to put together the many parts of the machine was as **intricate** as the machine itself.*

Synonyms: complicated, involved; complex, perplexing

a looking inward at one's own thoughts and feelings

*She sat in **introspection** at the piano recital, remembering her own days as a piano student.*

Synonyms: contemplation, reflection

IRONY
(AHY-ruh-nee)

IRREVERENT
(ih-REV-er-uhnt)

the use of words to express the opposite of their literal meaning; a difference between what is expected and the actual result

*The **irony** of the fate of Oedipus is that the very actions his parents took to evade the oracle's prediction were the actions that made it possible for her prediction to come true.*

Synonym: incongruity

• •

without proper respect or seriousness

*He was soon discharged from the military, because he could not tame his **irreverent** behavior.*

Synonyms: flippant, impertinent, impudent, mocking

• •

JAUNTY
(JAWN-tee)

JEJUNE
(ji-JOON)

JOVIAL
(JOH-vee-uhl)

lively in manner or appearance

*The arrival of spring inspired her warm smile and **jaunty** step.*

Synonyms: sprightly, vivacious

• •

without interest or importance; immature; uninformed

*The open mike at the coffee shop was usually tedious, featuring the **jejune** efforts of locals who fancied themselves songwriters or poets.*

Synonyms: dull, insipid; juvenile, childish

• •

characterized by jollity and hearty good nature

*His **jovial** mood lifted everyone's spirits.*

Synonyms: convivial, merry

J

JUDICIOUS

(joo-DISH-uhs)

J

characterized by good judgment

*Through the **judicious** use of the funds, she was able to complete the project on the very small budget allotted to her.*

Synonyms: prudent, sensible, wise

• •

KIN
(kin)

KINETIC
(ki-NET-ik or *kuh-NET-ik)*

KOWTOW
(KOW-tow or *kow-TOW)*

one's relatives; a group of people sharing a common ancestor

After the death of her parents, her nearest ***kin*** *were a few cousins whom she had never met.*

Synonyms: family; clan, kindred

• •

having to do with movement and the energy associated with movement; active, dynamic

Such ***kinetic*** *activities as running and dancing energize some people and tire others.*

Synonyms: active, dynamic

• •

to show deference; to show respect or worship by kneeling and touching the forehead to the ground

I don't understand why she's so popular; she expects everyone to ***kowtow*** *to her and take care of her every little desire.*

Synonyms: fawn; prostrate

LABYRINTH
(LAB-uh-rinth)

LACONIC
(luh-KON-ik)

LAISSEZ-FAIRE
(le-sey-FAIR or *le-zey-FAIR)*

a complex set of paths or passages, in which one is easily lost; a maze constructed of high hedges; a confusing or intricate arrangement or state of affairs

*Our new office building was such a poorly designed **labyrinth** that it took most of us at least a month to find our way around.*

Synonyms: maze, tangle

using few words

*His **laconic** responses to our questions provided so little information as to be useless.*

Synonyms: brusque, concise, succinct

(*n.*) a doctrine opposing the involvement of government in economic affairs; a philosophy opposing any interference in the affairs of others, particularly in regard to individual freedoms

(*adj.*) having to do with the ideas or practices of laissez-faire

*Her **laissez-faire** attitude conveyed not indifference but a deep sense of trust in the choices her students would make, if given the opportunity to choose.*

Synonyms: indifferent; hands-off

LAMPOON
(lam-POON)

LANGUID
(LAN-gwid)

LATENT
(LEY-tnt)

(*n.*) a satire, usually directed at an individual

The story that Harold published in the school newspaper was a thinly veiled ***lampoon*** *of the principal—which everyone but the principal enjoyed.*

Synonyms: burlesque, caricature

(*v.*) to ridicule

In the show, the comedians ***lampooned*** *everyone from world leaders to members of the audience.*

Synonyms: mock, parody

lacking energy or spirit; drooping from fatigue

She loves August, when the ***languid*** *days of summer give way to cooler evenings and the promise of a crisp, invigorating fall.*

Synonyms: indifferent, listless, slack; sluggish, weak

present as a possibility but not yet apparent or active

I love late February and early March, when the ***latent*** *promise of spring is just about ready to burst forth.*

Synonyms: dormant, potential

L

LATTER
(LAT-er)

• •

LETHARGY
(LETH-er-jee)

• •

LEXICON
(LEK-si-kon)

the second of two things or ideas mentioned; belonging to a later or more recent time or period

*Between rising early or staying up late to get the work done, I always choose the **latter**; if I'm not going to sleep much, I like at least to wake knowing that the task is already complete.*

Synonyms: last, later, recent, second

• •

drowsiness or laziness

*The cause of her **lethargy** that morning was not laziness but a terrible case of the flu.*

Synonyms: apathy, listlessness, stupor

• •

a book containing an alphabetized list of words and their definitions; the vocabulary in a language, known by a speaker or group of speakers, or having to do with a particular subject; an inventory or record

*In the entire **lexicon** of words having to do with the emotions, he could think of none that quite described the sense of hopeful longing he felt that day.*

Synonyms: dictionary, vocabulary

LICENTIOUS
(lahy-SEN-shuhs)

LISTLESS
(LIST-luhs)

LOATHE
(lohth)

without legal or moral restraints, especially sexual restraints; disregarding rules

*To indulge in such **licentious** behavior may be pleasurable, but it can also be dangerous, especially to your health.*

Synonyms: immoral, lascivious, lawless, libertine

without energy or spirit

*He greeted us with a **listless** handshake that inspired little confidence.*

Synonyms: indifferent, languid, spiritless

to dislike to the point of intolerance or disgust

*I **loathe** people who mock those who are weaker than themselves.*

Synonyms: abhor, despise, detest

LOQUACIOUS
(loh-KWEY-shuhs)

LUGUBRIOUS
(luh-GOO-bree-uhs)

LUMINOUS
(LOO-muh-nuhs)

tending to or characterized by excessive talk

*I'm certain that our neighbor is so **loquacious** whenever we see her simply because she gets lonely with no one to talk to during the day.*

Synonyms: talkative, verbose, wordy

• •

mournful, gloomy, often in an exaggerated way

*On Halloween, he wore a zombie costume and went about the neighborhood moaning in **lugubrious** tones.*

Synonyms: dismal, woebegone

• •

illuminated in or shining with light

*The pond shimmered in the **luminous** glow of the full moon that night.*

Synonyms: bright, brilliant, glowing, radiant, shining

L

LURID
(LOOR-id)

ACT VOCABULARY

gruesome, shocking, or unrestrained; lit with a garish or fiery glow; wan

*Please keep the **lurid** details of your accident to yourself, at least while I'm eating my lunch.*

Synonyms: horrible, revolting, sensational

MALADY
(MAL-uh-dee)

MALEVOLENT
(muh-LEV-uh-luhnt)

MAMMOTH
(MAM-uhth)

an illness or disease

The doctors were unable to find a diagnosis for the ***malady*** *that had him bedridden for a week.*

Synonyms: affliction, disorder

• •

characterized by ill will or hatred

In the haunted house, the children cowered at the ***malevolent*** *cackle of the witch.*

Synonyms: evil, hateful, vicious, vindictive

• •

great in size

Typically weighing some 150 tons, the blue whale is truly a ***mammoth*** *creature.*

Synonyms: enormous, giant, gigantic, huge

M

MANEUVER
(muh-NOO-vuhr)

MANIFEST
(MAN-uh-fest)

ACT VOCABULARY

(*n.*) a military movement or training exercise; a method of working or a technique that involves physical skill; an action taken to trick or for tactical gain

*With one quick **maneuver** he dislodged the broken part from the machine.*

Synonyms: contrivance, manipulation, stratagem

(*v.*) to take an action for tactical gain, to scheme; to bring about by maneuvers, to manipulate

*She **maneuvered** her way through the crowd and managed to claim a seat in the front row.*

Synonyms: contrive, finagle

• •

(*adj.*) easily perceived or understood, obvious

*His distress about leaving home was **manifest** in his slouching gait and furrowed brow.*

Synonyms: apparent, evident, plain

(*v.*) to make evident

*She **manifested** her delight by jumping up and down and clapping.*

Synonyms: demonstrate, illustrate, substantiate

• •

M

MARSUPIAL
(mar-SOO-pee-uhl)

MAUDLIN
(MAWD-lin)

MAWKISH
(MAW-kish)

a mammal whose females do not develop a true placenta and typically have a pouch for carrying young

Australian wildlife is dominated by a wide variety of ***marsupials****, including kangaroos, koalas, and wombats.*

weakly sentimental or tearful; sentimental because of drunkenness

The teacher was unmoved by the student's ***maudlin*** *tale of his lost homework.*

Synonym: insipid

insipid, sentimental

With its ***mawkish*** *tone and clichéd plot, this book is just silly.*

Synonym: maudlin

MEAGER
(MEE-guhr)

MEASURED
(MEZH-erd)

MEGALOMANIA
(meg-uh-loh-MEY-nee-uh)

lacking in quality or quantity; thin

*His **meager** salary barely covered his rent and other living expenses.*

Synonyms: deficient, inadequate, scanty, sparse

determined or apportioned by measure; regular or rhythmical; deliberate and restrained

*He gave **measured** replies to their heated questions and gradually calmed the crowd.*

Synonyms: calculated; uniform; careful

a mania for doing grand or extravagant things

*Driven more by **megalomania** than a desire to serve, he sought to become president.*

Synonyms: vanity, conceit; narcissism

MELANCHOLY
(MEL-uhn-kol-ee)

• •

MELLIFLUOUS
(muh-LIF-loo-uhs)

• •

METAMORPHOSIS
(met-uh-MOUR-fuh-sis)

(*n.*) a state of depression or low spirits

*I often cannot shake the **melancholy** of the winter months until we are well into spring.*

Synonyms: despondency, gloom

(*adj.*) sorrowful, depressed, or causing sorrow or depression

*Our sprits sank as we listened to his **melancholy** tale.*

Synonyms: despondent, gloomy, unhappy

• •

smoothly and richly flowing; sweetened as with honey

*Only the **mellifluous** song of a nightingale broke the silence of the forest.*

Synonyms: dulcet, melodious, soothing

• •

a change in physical form, substance, or character, often through supernatural means

*The coming of spring worked a **metamorphosis** over the landscape, and the trees that had seemed barren just a week earlier were laden with pink blossoms.*

Synonyms: mutation, rebirth, transformation

MIRTH
(muhrth)

MISANTHROPE
(MIS-uhn-throhp)

MISNOMER
(mis-NOH-mer)

gaiety accompanied by laughter

*The children could not contain their **mirth** at the cleverly ridiculous play.*

Synonyms: happiness, merriment

• •

one who tends to dislike or distrust humanity

*A **misanthrope**, she lived alone with her half-dozen cats and rarely spoke to others.*

Synonyms: cynic, skeptic

• •

a wrong or inappropriate name or designation

*The term "koala bear" is a **misnomer** because koalas are not actually bears.*

MISSIVE
(MIS-iv)

MOIETY
(MOI-i-tee)

MOLLIFY
(MOL-uh-fahy)

a written message

*A **missive** full of unsolicited advice from her parents arrived in her mailbox every week.*

Synonym: letter

• •

one half; one portion or share

*This basket of apples is just a **moiety** of all that we harvested today.*

Synonyms: part, piece

• •

to soften the temper or feeling

*To **mollify** their customers, the store replaced the defective boots for free.*

Synonyms: appease, mellow, mitigate, pacify, placate

MORASS
(muh-RAS)

MOROSE
(muh-ROHS)

MOSAIC
(moh-ZEY-ik)

a swamp; a confusing or difficult situation

*His term paper was a **morass** of inconsequential details, presented with no thesis.*

Synonyms: bog, marsh, quagmire; entanglement

• •

gloomy, sullen

*We took one look at his **morose** face and knew that the team had lost.*

Synonyms: ill-humored, melancholy

• •

a picture or design made by inlaying small pieces of differently colored materials, such as glass, stone, or tile; something made of diverse elements

*Many of the subway stations in Manhattan are decorated with colorful **mosaics**.*

Synonyms: collage; motley

MUTABLE
(MYOO-tuh-buhl)

MUTATION
(myoo-TEY-shuhn)

MYOPIC
(mahy-OP-ik)

subject to change

*His moods were as **mutable** as the weather.*

Synonyms: fickle, inconstant, unreliable

a change in hereditary material, such as chromosomes or genes; a change in the nature or form or something

*The disease was found to be the result of a **mutation** in a gene.*

Synonym: transformation

having myopia, nearsighted; short-sighted or narrow-minded

*Their decision to cut funding for preschool programs was **myopic** because such programs have been shown to have a positive effect on the lives of their students, even in adulthood.*

Synonyms: blind, intolerant

NADIR
(NEY-dir)

NASCENT
(NEY-suhnt or NAS-uhnt)

NEFARIOUS
(ni-FAIR-ee-uhs)

ACT VOCABULARY

the lowest point

*My energy and mood were at their **nadir**, and so I decided to take a nap.*

Synonyms: base, bottom

• •

just coming into existence

*Seeing that the trees were beginning to bud, I became giddy at the very thought of the **nascent** spring.*

Synonyms: burgeoning, fledgling, incipient

• •

wicked or vicious

*Her **nefarious** plot to destroy the company was discovered and foiled.*

Synonyms: evil, treacherous, villainous

N

NOISOME
(NOI-suhm)

NOSTALGIA
(nuh-STAL-juh)

NOXIOUS
(NOK-shuhs)

harmful; offensive to the senses, especially smell; obnoxious

*It would have been a lovely neighborhood if it were not for the **noisome** odors sometimes emitted from a nearby factory.*

Synonyms: noxious; disgusting, repulsive

• •

a state of longing for the past

*He was almost overwhelmed with **nostalgia** when the band played the song his grandmother sang to him when he was a child.*

Synonyms: homesickness, longing, yearning

• •

poisonous or corrupting

*The chemists covered themselves with masks, gloves, and heavy smocks to protect themselves from the **noxious** fumes.*

Synonyms: deadly, injurious, harmful, pernicious, toxic

OBFUSCATE
(OB-fuh-skeyt)

OBSOLETE
(ob-suh-LEET)

OBSTINATE
(OB-stuh-nit)

to confuse or make obscure

The more he said, the more he ***obfuscated*** *the truth, which was really quite simple.*

Synonyms: baffle, bewilder, conceal, perplex

• •

no longer in use, useful, or current

New technologies are developed so quickly now that old ones can become ***obsolete*** *within a matter of just a few years.*

Synonyms: antiquated, archaic

• •

persistent in a belief or behavior; not easily remedied, changed, or controlled

The ***obstinate*** *young man refused to compromise, and so he was left with nothing.*

Synonyms: determined, dogged, stubborn, unyielding

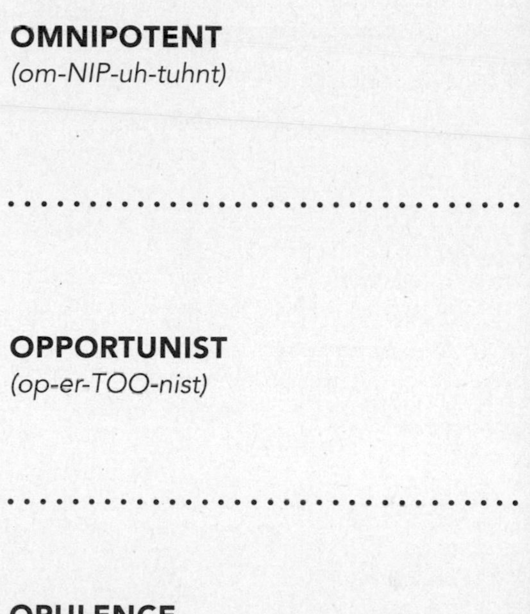

OMNIPOTENT
(om-NIP-uh-tuhnt)

OPPORTUNIST
(op-er-TOO-nist)

OPULENCE
(OP-yuh-luhns)

having unlimited power or authority

*Very young children typically believe that their parents are **omnipotent**.*

Synonyms: almighty, all-powerful

• •

one who takes advantage of opportunities with little thought for principles or consequences

*She was an **opportunist** who cared much less about friendship than she did about knowing all the right people in all the right places.*

• •

wealth; abundance

*The **opulence** on display at the royal banquet was overwhelming.*

Synonyms: affluence, prosperity, riches; plenty

O

ORNERY
(AWR-nuh-ree)

OSTENTATIOUS
(os-ten-TEY-shuhs)

OSTRACIZE
(OS-truh-sahyz)

having an unpleasant disposition, stubborn

*Don't be so **ornery** with your sister! She's just trying to help.*

Synonyms: cantankerous, difficult

• •

characterized by showy or pretentious display

*He tended to be **ostentatious** in his generosity, which led me to believe that this philanthropy had a lot to do with needing the approval of others.*

Synonyms: conspicuous, extravagant, flamboyant, flashy

• •

to exclude from a group by general consent

*He was **ostracized** by his classmates after he was found to be the one responsible for the vandalism.*

Synonyms: avoid, isolate, reject

OUST
(owst)

to remove from a position or place, either legally or by force

*In an attempt to **oust** the prime minister, the assembly brought down the government through a vote of no confidence.*

Synonyms: banish, eject, evict

PAINSTAKING
(PEYN-stey-king)

PALLID
(PAL-id)

PALPABLE
(PAL-puh-buhl)

taking pains: that is, taking great care and effort

*Taking **painstaking** care with the details, the conservator restored the painting so beautifully that you would never know it had been damaged.*

Synonyms: diligent, conscientious, particular

• •

lacking color or energy

*Janice was well enough to get out of bed, but her **pallid** face showed that she was still not completely healthy.*

Synonyms: dull, pale, wan

• •

capable of being felt, tangible; readily perceived

*Her relief at hearing the good news was **palpable**; she sighed and then smiled as I had not seen her smile for weeks.*

Synonyms: conspicuous, evident, obvious

PARIAH
(puh-RAHY-uh)

PAROCHIAL
(puh-ROH-kee-uhl)

PEDESTRIAN
(puh-DES-tree-uhn)

someone who is despised or rejected

*Once they found out she had been lying the whole time, they treated her like a **pariah**, refusing to talk with her or even to look at her.*

Synonyms: outcast, undesirable

• •

having to do with a parish; confined (as though to a parish), limited in outlook or scope

*You are going to have to let go of your **parochial** mentality if you are going to thrive here in the big city.*

Synonyms: insular, provincial

• •

ordinary, unimaginative

*The extravagant sets and costumes are not going to disguise the **pedestrian** plot of this play.*

Synonyms: commonplace, dull, mediocre, mundane, prosaic

PERFUNCTORY
(puhr-FUHNGK-tuh-ree)

PERNICIOUS
(puhr-NISH-uhs)

PINNACLE
(PIN-uh-kuhl)

done in a routine, superficial, or indifferent way

*Their **perfunctory** work showed just how little they cared about the project or its success.*

Synonyms: automatic, mechanical, offhand, unthinking

• •

destructive or deadly

*Smoking is a **pernicious** habit that unfortunately is extraordinarily difficult to break.*

Synonyms: detrimental, harmful, injurious, noxious, ruinous

• •

a high peak; the highest point

*Her joy was at its **pinnacle** when it was announced that her team would be representing the state at the national competition.*

Synonyms: climax, summit, zenith

PIOUS
(PAHY-uhs)

PITHY
(PITH-ee)

PLACEBO
(pluh-SEE-boh)

characterized by religious devotion or by conspicuous and hypocritical virtue

*His **pious** appearance had little to do with his character, and it was discovered that his regular attendance at services was due to a scheme to defraud the church.*

Synonyms: devout, religious, reverent, righteous, sanctimonious, scrupulous

• •

brief and meaningful

*Her **pithy** observations were both accurate and funny.*

Synonyms: cogent, expressive, pointed, succinct, terse

• •

an inert substance used in place of a medicine, either given to relieve a patient who does not know that it is not a medicine or used as a control in a study

*I do not know whether the pill was a **placebo** or an actual medication, but its effect was certain: My mother said she felt better almost immediately.*

Synonym: sugar pill

PLATITUDE
(PLAT-i-tood)

PLIANT
(PLAHY-uhnt)

PLUCKY
(PLUHK-ee)

a banal or trite statement

The counselor did not listen well, and she gave the students ***platitudes*** *such as "Look before you leap!" instead of useful advice.*

Synonyms: commonplace, cliché

• •

easily bent; easily influenced

Learn to assert yourself with your peers; don't be so ***pliant****!*

Synonyms: adaptable, flexible, supple; compliant, manageable, yielding

• •

spirited or courageous

The ***plucky*** *young woman marched right up to the principal and made her demands.*

Synonyms: confident, tenacious, undaunted

PLUMMET
(PLUHM-it)

PONDEROUS
(PON-der-uhs)

PORTENTOUS
(pour-TEN-tuhs or pohr-TEN-tuhs)

to fall or drop sharply and suddenly

*The skydiver **plummeted** from the plane and then opened his parachute.*

Synonyms: collapse, plunge

• •

heavy; unwieldy due to weight; dull

*It was a **ponderous** tome in both heft and style.*

Synonyms: massive; awkward, burdensome; labored, lifeless

• •

having to do with or giving a portent or omen; gravely significant; marvelous

*The **portentous** tone of his speech was completely uncalled for, as virtually nothing he predicted actually came to pass.*

Synonyms: extraordinary, momentous

P

PORTLY
(POURT-lee)

PRAGMATIC
(prag-MAT-ik)

PRECARIOUS
(pri-KAIR-ee-uhs)

heavy; stately

*The **portly** actor was cast as Santa Claus.*

Synonyms: ample, corpulent, stout; dignified

oriented toward the practical

*We were **pragmatic** about our limited budget, so rather than spend money on travel, we stayed home for our vacation.*

Synonyms: businesslike, efficient, realistic, utilitarian

dependent on uncertain or chance circumstances

*That's a **precarious** place to put that vase—why don't you put it on a sturdier table?*

Synonyms: contingent, insecure, perilous, shaky, unreliable

P

PRECOCIOUS
(pri-KOH-shuhs)

PREDICAMENT
(pri-DIK-uh-muhnt)

PRESUMPTUOUS
(pri-ZUHMP-choo-uhs)

unusually mature or advanced early in development

***Precocious** from a young age, she was ready for college by the time she was fourteen.*

Synonym: advanced

• •

a difficult situation

*He began to believe that the best way out of his **predicament** would be to leave town and start over somewhere else.*

Synonyms: condition, hardship

• •

overstepping bounds, such as of courtesy

*I'm sorry; it was **presumptuous** of me to invite myself to your party.*

Synonyms: audacious, bold, overconfident

P

PRETENTIOUS
(pri-TEN-shuhs)

PROFICIENT
(pruh-FISH-uhnt)

PROLIFIC
(pruh-LIF-ik)

making an show of one's importance, dignity, or achievements

*His **pretentious** manners put off those whom he intended to impress.*

Synonyms: grandiloquent, ostentatious, showy, vainglorious

• •

having advanced skill

*A **proficient** athlete, she was successful at many sports.*

Synonyms: accomplished, consummate, experienced

• •

abundantly productive, fertile

*He was a **prolific** musician, pursuing several collaborations at once while also writing and recording at least one solo album per year.*

Synonyms: bountiful, fruitful, teeming

PROPONENT
(pruh-POH-nuhnt)

• •

PROSAIC
(proh-ZEY-ik)

• •

PROSPERITY
(pro-SPER-i-tee)

one who argues in favor of something or supports a cause

*I'm not the only **proponent** of the new law; I'm just the only vocal one.*

Synonyms: adherent, advocate, champion, supporter

• •

like prose, rather than like poetry; dull, factual

*After my adventures abroad, I'm looking forward to leading a more **prosaic** life at home.*

Synonyms: commonplace, unimaginative

• •

a condition of success, especially economic well-being

*Believing that his **prosperity** would not have been possible without the help of others, he was generous with his wealth.*

Synonyms: abundance, advantage

PROVINCIAL
(pruh-VIN-shuhl)

PRUDENT
(PROO-dnt)

PUDGY
(PUHJ-ee)

limited in outlook, unsophisticated

*New Yorkers can actually be quite **provincial**, acting as though nothing worthwhile exists beyond the island of Manhattan.*

Synonyms: insular, parochial

• •

wise or careful in practical matters

*Allison was **prudent** with her money, and by the end of the year she had saved enough for a cross-country trip.*

Synonyms: discerning, judicious, sagacious, sober

• •

short and plump

*He was a **pudgy** baby, with dimples at his elbows and knees.*

Synonym: chubby

P

PUERILE
(PYOOR-il or *PYOOR-ahyl)*

PUGNACIOUS
(puhg-NEY-shuhs)

PUNGENT
(PUHN-juhnt)

childish, immature

*"You are far too old for such **puerile** behavior," said the teacher to the student who had shot the spitball.*

Synonyms: juvenile, trivial

• •

tending to quarrel or fight

*He was both **pugnacious** and foolish, constantly picking fights with people much bigger and stronger than he.*

Synonyms: belligerent, combative, quarrelsome

• •

sharp, painful, to the point

*His **pungent** reply invited no further questions or comments.*

Synonyms: acrid, biting, caustic

QUANDARY
(KWAN-dree)

QUELL
(kwel)

QUERULOUS
(KWER-uh-luhs)

a state of confusion or uncertainty

*After our first experiment failed unexpectedly, we were in a **quandary** about what to do next.*

Synonyms: dilemma, impasse, predicament

• •

to put an end to, subdue, or quiet

*Our uncle told us funny stories in order to **quell** our fears of the ferocious storm.*

Synonyms: extinguish, overcome, vanquish

• •

given to complaining

*The **querulous** old woman bored them with complaints about her arthritis and ungrateful children.*

Synonyms: dissatisfied, fretful, whining

Q

QUERY
(KWEER-ee)

QUIXOTIC
(kwik-SOT-ik)

question

I had to submit my ***query*** *three times by e-mail before I received an answer.*

Synonym: question

extravagantly foolish or romantic in the pursuit of ideals

The mayor's ***quixotic*** *plan would not only have every town resident fully employed, he said, but enjoying a prosperous, middle-class lifestyle.*

Synonyms: chivalrous, impractical, visionary, utopian

RANCOR
(RANG-ker)

RANT
(rant)

RAPPORT
(ra-POUR)

deep ill will

*After their long and bitter argument, the former friends felt nothing but **rancor** toward each other.*

Synonyms: animosity, enmity, spite

• •

(v.) to speak loudly and wildly, often angrily

*Calm down and stop **ranting**! No one can understand what you are saying!*

Synonyms: declaim, rave

(n.) a loud, excited speech, often angry

*The teacher's **rant** startled the students and even frightened some of them.*

Synonym: diatribe

• •

relation, especially a sympathetic relation

*Believing that the best way to motivate the team was from a foundation of trust, the coach established a good **rapport** with the players at the beginning of the season.*

Synonyms: affinity, concord, harmony

R

RAPT
(rapt)

RASH
(rash)

RATIONAL
(RASH-uh-nuhl or *RASH-nuhl)*

ACT VOCABULARY

R

deeply absorbed; transported

*The magician held the **rapt** attention of the children.*

Synonyms: engrossed; enraptured

• •

hasty, done without thought or caution

*Upon later consideration, she realized that her **rash** decision to drop out of school had been foolish.*

Synonyms: impulsive, reckless

• •

based on or agreeable to reason; having or using reason or good sense; in mathematics, describing a number that can be represented by a ratio of two integers

*Though the plan looked **rational** on paper, problems arose as soon as we began to carry it through.*

Synonyms: reasonable, sensible

RAUCOUS
(RAW-kuhs)

RAVENOUS
(RAV-uh-nuhs)

RECANT
(ri-KANT)

strident; rowdy and disorderly

*The party got so **raucous** that the neighbors called the police.*

Synonyms: cacophonous, harsh, grating; boisterous

extremely hungry or eager for food or satisfaction

*She was **ravenous** after she finished the marathon.*

Synonyms: famished, voracious; insatiable, rapacious

to openly and formally withdraw or disavow a statement or belief

*They threatened to sue the newspaper if it would not **recant** what they said were libelous accusations.*

Synonyms: nullify, retract, void

RECEPTIVE
(ri-SEP-tiv)

RECLUSE
(REK-loos)

RECTIFY
(REK-tuh-fahy)

able to receive or open to receiving, especially new ideas

*At the festival, they found a **receptive** audience for their music.*

Synonyms: accessible, open-minded

• •

one who has withdrawn from society

*It is rumored that a **recluse** lives in the woods here, but I have never seen him.*

Synonym: hermit

• •

to set right or correct

*The best way to **rectify** our situation is to review our classroom rules and change the ones that are not serving us well.*

Synonyms: adjust, redress, remedy

REFORM
(ri-FOURM)

REJUVENATE
(ri-JOO-vuh-neyt)

RELISH
(REL-ish)

to improve that which is corrupt, to change for the better, to put an end to troubles or abuses

*If elected, I promise to **reform** the schools so that all of our students are learning.*

Synonyms: renovate, transform

• •

to make young or like young again, to restore to an earlier state

***Rejuvenated** by his vacation, he looked like a young man again.*

Synonyms: refresh, revitalize

• •

(*n.*) pleasure, enjoyment

*She played the guitar with **relish** and enchanted everyone with her fervor.*

(*v.*) to enjoy

*"Believe me, I do not **relish** the idea of giving you this test," said the teacher, "because after all, I'll have to take the time to evaluate and grade it."*

Synonym: delight

R

REMUNERATION
(ri-myoo-nuh-REY-shuhn)

RENOWN
(ri-NOUN)

REPLICATE
(REP-li-keyt)

something that pays in kind; the act or fact of paying in kind

*She neither asked for nor received any **remuneration** for her efforts to find the lost child.*

Synonyms: compensation, pay, reward

• •

the state of being widely known and acclaimed

*Her **renown** was primarily among other archaeologists; the wider public knew little of her and her work.*

Synonyms: celebrity, fame, prestige, prominence

• •

to repeat or make a copy of

*We must have made a mistake in the original experiment, because we have never been able to **replicate** its results.*

Synonyms: duplicate, reproduce

REPUDIATE
(ri-PYOO-dee-eyt)

RESIGNED
(ri-ZAHYND)

RESILIENT
(ri-ZIL-yuhnt)

to disown or reject

*Though she could not completely **repudiate** her mother, Helen maintained her distance from her.*

Synonyms: condemn, disown, renounce

• •

submissive, having given up

*We protested at first, but eventually we were **resigned** to the fact that the volleyball team was going to be cut after one last season due to the shrinking school budget.*

Synonym: acquiescent

• •

elastic, able to return to its original shape after being compressed, stretched, or bent; able to adjust to change or recover from misfortune

*Children are **resilient**; your son will adjust to these changes, difficult as they may be, especially if you are honest with him.*

Synonym: flexible

RESTRAINED
(ri-STREYND)

RETICENT
(RET-uh-suhnt)

REVELRY
(REV-uhl-ree)

held back, not emotionally expressive or extravagant

She was so emotionally ***restrained*** *that you would not know that she was in mourning for her husband.*

Synonyms: controlled, reasonable, tasteful, temperate

• •

tending to be uncommunicative or silent

George is shy and tends to become ***reticent*** *among strangers.*

Synonyms: reserved, restrained

• •

joyful, noisy celebration

The wedding party invited us to join in their ***revelry****.*

Synonyms: festivity, gaiety

REVILE
(ri-VAHYL)

• •

REVITALIZE
(ree-VAHYT-uhl-ahyz)

• •

REVULSION
(ri-VUHL-shuhn)

to assail with verbal abuse or to speak of with abuse

*Though his films were **reviled** by critics, the movie director did not care; most of them were blockbusters that had made him a lot of money.*

Synonyms: berate, criticize, rail, reprimand, scold

• •

to give new life to, to invigorate

*The coach's halftime speech inspired the team, and they returned to the field **revitalized** for the second half of the game.*

Synonyms: exhilarate, rejuvenate, replenish

• •

disgust; a sudden change in feeling; the act of drawing or pulling away

*I was filled with sorrow and **revulsion** when she described how she had been abused.*

Synonyms: aversion, distaste, loathing, repugnance

R

RIBALD
(RIB-uhld)

RUMINATE
(ROO-muh-neyt)

RUSTIC
(RUHS-tik)

characterized by crude or irreverent speech or humor

*The comedian is known for his **ribald** humor, so you might want to skip the show if you're easily offended.*

Synonyms: coarse, indecent, vulgar

• •

to go over again and again in the mind, to reflect; literally, to chew on repeatedly

*The philosophy professor recommended that we go over our assignments slowly, reading just one paragraph at a time and **ruminating** on its meaning before reading the next one.*

Synonyms: contemplate, muse, ponder

• •

of or related to the country; plain or unsophisticated

*Their home was filled with **rustic** furniture, as though they lived in a farmhouse instead of an apartment in the city.*

Synonyms: rural; provincial, simple, unaffected

SACCHARINE
(SAK-er-in)

SALIENT
(SEY-lyuhnt or *SEY-lee-uhnt)*

SANCTIMONIOUS
(sangk-tuh-MOH-nee-uhs)

S

related to sugar or like sugar; overly sweet, agreeable, or sentimental

*Her **saccharine** manner with the children betrayed her lack of understanding of how to interact with them*

Synonyms: sugary; cloying, ingratiating

• •

standing out, prominent; projecting outward; leaping or jumping

*The most **salient** point in his long speech was his belief that the bill should be passed soon.*

Synonyms: notable, pronounced, significant

• •

hypocritically righteous, pious, or devout

*Spare me your **sanctimonious** judgments; I know that you have committed similar transgressions yourself.*

Synonyms: smug, unctuous

S

SANGUINE
(SANG-gwin)

SARDONIC
(sahr-DON-ik)

SATIATE
(SEY-shee-eyt)

optimistic, confident; ruddy

*Her **sanguine** attitude was infectious, and all of us soon felt hopeful about our chances of winning the tournament.*

Synonyms: assured, cheerful, enthusiastic, positive

disdainfully or skeptically humorous or mocking

*His openly **sardonic** attitude toward his teachers even rubbed his classmates the wrong way.*

Synonyms: cynical, scornful, sneering

to satisfy fully or supply to excess

*If the meal did not **satiate** your appetite, this dessert certainly will.*

Synonyms: fill, gratify, indulge

SAVORY
(SEY-vuh-ree)

. . . .

SCRIBE
(skrahyb)

. . . .

SECRETE
(si-KREET)

pleasant in taste, especially due to seasoning and without sweetness; piquant; pleasing

*My mouth began to water at the very thought of the **savory** dishes—meatloaf and mashed potatoes—that were being prepared in the kitchen.*

Synonyms: delectable, palatable

• •

one who copies manuscripts; an official or public clerk, secretary, or writer

*Before the invention of the printing press, **scribes** copied books by hand.*

Synonyms: copyist, transcriber

• •

to give off or release a substance or secretion such as sweat

*The pancreas **secretes** such hormones as insulin as well as digestive enzymes.*

Synonyms: discharge, emit

S

SEDATIVE
(SED-uh-tiv)

SEDENTARY
(SED-n-ter-ee)

SEDITION
(si-DISH-uhn)

(*adj.*) tending to calm

I am far too wound up to feel the ***sedative*** *effects of this herbal tea.*

Synonyms: calming, relaxing, soothing

(*n.*) a calming agent or drug

They gave the cat a ***sedative*** *so that it would tolerate the long car trip.*

Synonym: tranquilizer

• •

doing or requiring a lot of sitting, not physically active

Because they spend so much time watching TV or playing video games, many children have a much more ***sedentary*** *lifestyle than did children in the past.*

Synonym: inactive

• •

incitement of rebellion against a government

The editor of the newspaper was accused of ***sedition*** *for publishing articles that were harshly critical of the government.*

Synonyms: dissent, revolution, treason

SEMINAL
(SEM-uh-nl)

SEQUESTER
(si-KWES-ter)

SERENDIPITY
(ser-uhn-DIP-i-tee)

providing the seeds of later development

Completed in 1950, Jackson Pollock's Autumn Rhythm *is a **seminal** work of postwar abstraction.*

Synonyms: influential, original

• •

to set apart or withdraw

*The jury will be **sequestered** in this hotel until they have reached a verdict.*

Synonyms: seclude, segregate

• •

an aptitude for or the phenomenon of coming upon good or valuable things by accident, or an instance of such a finding

*He claimed that his success was due to **serendipity**, but I believe that his hard work helped him find luck.*

Synonyms: happenstance, luck

SERENITY
(suh-REN-i-tee)

SERVILE
(SUR-vahyl)

SLOVENLY
(SLUHV-uhn-lee)

S

the state of being serene or peaceful

*We were accustomed to the hubbub of city life, and so the **serenity** of the mountains was unbelievably delightful to us.*

Synonyms: calmness, tranquility

• •

submissive, like a slave

*Behind their **servile** manners, the servants hid their true contempt for their boss.*

Synonyms: abject, obedient, subservient

• •

untidy or dirty in appearance or habits

*Because of his brilliant thinking, the professor's colleagues tended to overlook his **slovenly** appearance.*

Synonyms: careless, disheveled, negligent, sloppy, unkempt

S

SOJOURN
(SOH-juhrn)

SOLICITOUS
(suh-LIS-i-tuhs)

SONOROUS
(suh-NAWR-uhs or *SON-er-uhs)*

S

a temporary stay or residence

*He finished writing his novel during a month-long **sojourn** by the ocean.*

Synonyms: visit, stopover

• •

showing concern or care; eager

*Though she recognized that they were trying to help, she refused to respond to their **solicitous** questions.*

Synonyms: anxious, attentive, careful, worried

• •

producing sound, especially a resonant sound; loud or rich in sound

*The poet read his work in a **sonorous** voice that filled every corner of the theater.*

Synonyms: resounding, rich

SOPHISTRY
(SOF-uh-stree)

SOPHOMORIC
(sof-MOR-ik)

SPARTAN
(SPAHR-tn)

S

deceptive reasoning, a false argument

*The **sophistry** of the ad campaign was evident; however, many people were hoodwinked into buying the product.*

Synonyms: deception, fallacy, misconception

• •

pretentious or overconfident while being immature

*Unfortunately, he continued to behave in this **sophomoric** fashion well into his twenties.*

Synonyms: foolish, naïve

• •

severely disciplined and simple; courageous

*She approached her studies with a **spartan** rigor that served her well through college and graduate school.*

Synonyms: austere, rigorous

SPONTANEOUS
(spon-TEY-nee-uhs)

• •

SPURIOUS
(SPYOOR-ee-uhs)

• •

SPURN
(spuhrn)

arising from impulse, without planning or restraint; tending to act upon impulse

*Our decision to go to the beach today was **spontaneous**; we had actually been planning to work in the garden.*

Synonyms: extemporaneous, uncontrolled

• •

not genuine or true

*His reason for declining the invitation may have been **spurious**, but it was meant to spare their feelings.*

Synonyms: contrived, counterfeit, deceitful, deceptive

• •

to reject with disdain

*She **spurns** that restaurant, claiming that its kitchen is infested with pests.*

Synonym: scorn

S

SQUALID
(SKWOL-id or *SKWAW-lid)*

STAGNANT
(STAG-nuhnt)

STOIC
(STOH-ik)

ACT VOCABULARY

filthy from neglect or poverty

*The family lived in **squalid** conditions at the outskirts of the city until they could afford a decent apartment.*

Synonyms: disgusting, miserable, sordid

• •

not flowing or moving, as of air or water; stale; not developing

*The apartment windows had been shut for weeks, and the **stagnant** air smelled foul.*

Synonyms: inactive, lifeless, standing, stationary

• •

(*adj.*) not showing feeling

*His **stoic** response to the loss of their home helped his family recover from the tragedy.*

Synonyms: dispassionate, indifferent, philosophic, self-controlled

(*n.*) one who seems to be indifferent to both pleasure and pain

*She prided herself for being a **stoic**, but I thought it would be healthier for her to allow herself to laugh or cry on occasion.*

S

STRATIFIED
(STRAT-uh-fahyd)

STRIDENT
(STRAHYD-nt)

STRINGENT
(STRIN-juhnt)

formed or arranged in layers or hierarchical classes

*The **stratified** cliffs provided a record of geological time that the archeologists could use to date their findings.*

Synonym: layered

• •

characterized by harsh and insistent sound, commanding attention

*Her **strident** voice broke through the noisy chatter of the children and caught their attention.*

Synonym: loud

• •

constricted; characterized by rigor or severity, particularly having to do with rules or standards

*Both faculty and staff are **stringent** in enforcing the many codes and rules at that school.*

Synonyms: tight; demanding, inflexible, severe, strict

SUBSISTENCE
(suhb-SIS-tuhns)

SUBTERRANEAN
(suhb-tuh-REY-nee-uhn)

SUBVERT
(suhb-VURT)

the state or fact of existing; the means of subsisting or provision of sustenance; the minimum needed to support life

Subsistence *farming provides just enough of the food and other goods that a family needs for its survival, with little or no surplus.*

Synonyms: means, support, sustenance

• •

underground, hidden

The movie featured the shady dealings of a ***subterranean*** *network of spies.*

Synonym: covert

• •

to overthrow or undermine

Their goal was to ***subvert*** *the government first by questioning the ethics of the president and then by impeaching him.*

Synonyms: contaminate, corrupt, destroy

S

SUCCESSIVE
(suhk-SES-iv)

SUCCINCT
(suhk-SINGKT)

SUCCUMB
(suh-KUHM)

following in order without interruption

The course will be run over five ***successive*** *Mondays.*

Synonyms: consecutive, sequential

• •

precise, using few words

Her ***succinct*** *reply told us everything we needed to know without confusing us with details.*

Synonyms: blunt, concise, pithy

• •

to yield to overpowering strength or persuasion; to give way to illness or old age and die

We ***succumbed*** *to his demands rather than expend our energy resisting him.*

Synonym: surrender

S

SUFFUSE
(suh-FYOOZ)

SULLEN
(SUHL-uhn)

SUPERSEDE
(soo-per-SEED)

to spread over or fill with or as with liquid or light

*At sunset, the lake and sky were both **suffused** with a pale golden light.*

Synonyms: permeate, saturate, spread

resentfully or gloomily silent; sluggish

*The **sullen** children perked up when they learned that the test would be postponed.*

Synonyms: dismal, gloomy, ill-humored, morose

to take the place or position of, displace

*This new set of rules and procedures **supersedes** those established by the former principal.*

Synonyms: replace, succeed, supplant

SUPPRESS
(suh-PRES)

SURFEIT
(SUR-fit)

SURMISE
(sur-MAHYZ)

to stop or keep down through authority or pressure, to keep secret

*The government attempted to **suppress** information about its illegal activities abroad.*

Synonyms: smother, conceal, withhold

• •

an excessive amount or indulgence in something

*The **surfeit** of food available at the cafeteria saddened her because she knew that much of it would ultimately go to waste.*

Synonyms: glut, overindulgence, satiety, surplus

• •

(*n.*) a guess

*Her **surmise** that they had eloped turned out to be true.*

Synonyms: conjecture, presumption, supposition

(*v.*) to infer without strong evidence

*She **surmised** that the reason for his absence was illness, but she had no way of knowing for certain.*

Synonyms: conjecture, guess, presume

S

SUSTAIN
(suh-STEYN)

• •

to support, bear, or keep up

You will not be able to ***sustain*** *this effort without nourishment and rest.*

Synonyms: buttress, continue, endure

TACIT
(TAS-it)

TACITURN
(TAS-i-turn)

TACT
(takt)

expressed or done without words, implied

I understood that we had come to a ***tacit*** *agreement when he winked.*

Synonyms: implicit, silent, suggested, unspoken

• •

tending to say little or be silent

His ***taciturn*** *ways intimidated me; I always felt that he was judging me in his silence.*

Synonyms: silent, reserved, reticent, withdrawn

• •

a keen sense of what should be said or done in order to avoid offending, particularly in difficult situations; good taste

I can't believe you didn't have the ***tact*** *to keep your mouth shut about his weight gain!*

Synonyms: poise, understanding

T

TACTILE
(TAK-til or *TAK-tahyl)*

TANGIBLE
(TAN-juh-buhl)

TARNISH
(TAHR-nish)

having to do with the sense of touch; capable of being touched

*The museum designed several **tactile** learning experiences for the children, who were encouraged to touch, hold, and even toss some of the objects in the exhibits.*

Synonyms: palpable, tangible

• •

capable of being touched, material; real, rather than imagined; definite

*He considered himself a realist and didn't believe in the existence of things that are neither visible nor **tangible**.*

Synonyms: corporeal, discernible, perceptible, substantial

• •

to make dull or to stain; to become dull or stained

*When it was revealed that she had been embezzling funds from the charity, not only was her reputation **tarnished**, but she lost her job and was eventually imprisoned.*

Synonyms: blemish, contaminate, discolor, sully

TAWDRY
(TAW-dree)

TEMPERANCE
(TEM-pruhns)

TEMPESTUOUS
(tem-PES-choo-uhs)

cheaply gaudy; base

*That **tawdry** gown may be appropriate for a Halloween costume, but certainly not for the charity banquet.*

Synonyms: brazen, vulgar

• •

moderation or restraint in thought, feeling, and deed; moderation in the indulgence of appetites or passions, particularly in the use of alcohol

*She never indulged in the excesses of her peers, and they admired her **temperance**.*

Synonyms: forbearance, self-control

• •

having to do with or similar to a storm

*Their **tempestuous** relationship was impossible to comprehend; one minute, they would be arguing and on the verge of a breakup, and the next minute, they would be proclaiming passionate love for each other.*

Synonyms: turbulent, stormy

TENACIOUS
(tuh-NEY-shuhs)

TENUOUS
(TEN-yoo-uhs)

TERRESTRIAL
(tuh-RES-tree-uhl)

holding fast, persistent; retentive, as in memory; holding together or adhesive

*The **tenacious** young man held on to his job even as his colleagues were quitting.*

Synonym: persevering

• •

thin in form or density; lacking substance, strength, clarity, or a sound basis in reasoning

*My understanding of physics was **tenuous**, and I failed the course.*

Synonyms: flimsy, questionable, unsubstantial, vague, weak

• •

of or related to the earth; of or related to land as distinguished from water; worldly or mundane

*Though they cannot fly, penguins are not wholly **terrestrial** birds; they are in fact elegant swimmers.*

Synonyms: earthbound, earthly; prosaic, secular

T

TERSE
(tuhrs)

THRESHOLD
(THRESH-hohld)

TIRADE
(TAHY-reyd)

concise, sometimes abruptly so

*My **terse** response may have seemed rude, but I'm not free to reveal any more information at this time.*

Synonyms: brief, curt, pithy, succinct

• •

the sill that lies under a door; a gate or point of entry, either literal or figurative

*Graduating from high school felt less like the conclusion of something than it did the **threshold** of a new and exciting life.*

Synonym: entrance

• •

a long and angry speech

*It is not appropriate to unleash such a **tirade** at children as young as they are; they will learn nothing but fear of your anger.*

Synonyms: diatribe, harangue, invective

T

TOLERANCE
(TOL-er-uhns)

TRANSCEND
(tran-SEND)

TRANSPIRE
(tran-SPAHYR)

the ability to endure; a fair or objective attitude toward those who are different from oneself (e.g., in race, nationality, or opinion); a fair or objective attitude toward different beliefs and practices

*I have no **tolerance** for dishonesty, and you will fail the course if I discover that you are cheating.*

Synonyms: endurance, fortitude, stamina; forbearance, sensitivity, understanding

• •

to rise above, overcome; to be independent of (time, material existence, etc.)

*Listening to music helped me to **transcend** my anxiety and complete the difficult project.*

Synonyms: exceed, outdo

• •

to take place; to be revealed or become known

*Very little has **transpired** since we last spoke; I have been busy with schoolwork and looking forward to vacation, and that is all.*

Synonyms: happen, occur; emerge

T

TRIFLING
(TRAHY-fling)

TROUPE
(troop)

insignificant or worthless

*The sum I owed was **trifling**, so it did not take long for me to pay it back.*

Synonyms: frivolous, negligible, trivial, unimportant

• •

a group, especially a group of performers

*She belonged to a dance **troupe** that toured the country every winter.*

Synonyms: band, company, ensemble

• •

UNCONSCIONABLE
(uhn-KON-shuh-nuh-buhl)

UNEQUIVOCAL
(uhn-i-KWIV-uh-kuhl)

UNHERALDED
(uhn-HER-uhl-did)

not guided by conscience; not just or reasonable; excessive

*It was an **unconscionable** decision to freeze the wages of most workers at the company while awarding large bonuses to upper management.*

Synonyms: unscrupulous; unreasonable; outrageous, preposterous

• •

leaving no doubt, having only one possible meaning, unqualified

*Ms. Ross was **unequivocal** about the deadline: She would be accepting no late term papers.*

Synonyms: absolute, clear, straightforward, unambiguous, unquestionable

• •

without fanfare or publicity, unannounced

***Unheralded** by either publicity or critical acclaim, the singer nevertheless steadily built an audience for her music.*

Synonyms: overlooked, unexpected, unknown, unnoticed

U

UNTENABLE
(uhn-TEN-uh-buhl)

UPBRAID
(up-BREYD)

USURP
(yoo-SURP)

incapable of being defended (describing an argument or belief); unsuitable for occupation (describing a building or apartment)

*The student assembly soon found that their position that all homework should be abolished was **untenable**, and so they decided to fight instead for a ban on homework over weekends and holidays.*

Synonyms: illogical, indefensible, unsound; uninhabitable

• •

to criticize severely, to scold

*My teacher **upbraided** me for forgetting the permission slip, and then I found it at the bottom of my book bag.*

Synonyms: censure, chastise, reprimand, reproach

• •

to take (an office, position, or authority) by force or without right; to use wrongfully or without right

*In the Glorious Revolution of 1688, the Dutch William of Orange **usurped** the English throne.*

Synonyms: displace, supplant, seize

U

UTILITARIAN
(yoo-til-i-TAIR-ee-uhn)

UTOPIA
(yoo-TOH-pee-uh)

characterized by or aimed at usefulness rather than beauty

*The design of his studio was plain and **utilitarian**; he wanted nothing there to distract him from his work.*

Synonyms: functional, pragmatic, sensible, useful

• •

a place or state of ideal perfection; a visionary scheme or system of political or social perfection

*Though you may dream of a **utopia** where all are equal and crime unheard of, I don't think that establishing such a place is possible, given human nature.*

Synonyms: Eden, paradise, Shangri-La, wonderland

• •

VACILLATE
(VAS-uh-leyt)

VAPID
(VAP-id)

VENERABLE
(VEN-er-uh-buhl or *VEN-ruh-buhl)*

to sway or fluctuate; to waver in feeling or hesitate in making a decision

Do not ***vacillate*** *between the two choices for too long because we need to know your decision by the end of the week.*

Synonyms: oscillate, stagger, swing; alternate, hedge, pause

• •

lacking energy or flavor

Bored with the ***vapid*** *conversation, I left the office party early.*

Synonyms: dull, flat, insipid, tedious

• •

respected by virtue of age, character, or accomplishments; hallowed because of religious or historical associations; impressive because of age

They turned to the ***venerable*** *diplomat to resolve their dispute.*

Synonyms: admirable, dignified, honorable, revered

V

VERACITY
(vuh-RAS-i-tee)

• •

VERBOSE
(ver-BOHS)

• •

VERDANT
(VUR-dnt)

truthfulness or accuracy

We will be calling your former employer to check the ***veracity*** *of your claims about your time there.*

Synonyms: authenticity, credibility, honesty

• •

tending to use more words than necessary, wordy

Her e-mails tend to be ***verbose****, but I always read them despite their length, because they also tend to be quite entertaining.*

Synonyms: garrulous, long-winded, loquacious

• •

green, especially with vegetation; inexperienced

After all the rain we've had this month, the lawns that had turned brown during the summer are ***verdant*** *again.*

Synonyms: flourishing, lush; unsophisticated

VICARIOUS
(vahy-KER-ee-uhs)

• •

VIE
(vahy)

• •

VIRILE
(VIR-uhl)

done or suffered in place of another; substituting for another person or thing; experienced through an imagined participation in the feelings or actions of another

*She disdains all forms of **vicarious** living, including watching television.*

Synonyms: surrogate, proxy

• •

to compete

*The two schools will **vie** for the state title at the track meet this weekend.*

Synonyms: challenge, contend, oppose, strive

• •

masculine, energetic

*Known for taking on **virile** roles as the lead in action-packed blockbusters, the actor surprised everyone with his latest film, a children's comedy in which he plays a clumsy suburban father.*

Synonyms: forceful, robust, strong, vigorous

VIRTUOSO
(vir-choo-OH-soh)

VIVID
(VIV-id)

VORACIOUS
(vaw-REY-shuhs)

(*n.*) one who excels at an art

*He was a **virtuoso** on the violin but clumsy in every other aspect of his life.*

Synonyms: genius, master, prodigy

(*adj.*) displaying excellence

*The audience applauded wildly at the conclusion of the symphony's **virtuoso** performance of Stravinsky's* The Rite of Spring.

Synonyms: masterful, skilled

• •

(of a color) very bright or intense; lively, realistic, distinct

*She gave such a **vivid** account of her trip that I could picture it as clearly as if I had been there with her myself.*

Synonyms: strong; energetic, expressive

• •

having a large appetite, insatiable

*A **voracious** reader, she often stayed up until the early hours of the morning to finish a novel.*

Synonyms: avid, gluttonous, ravenous

WAN
(won)

WARY
(WAIR-ee)

WHIMSICAL
(HWIM-zi-kuhl)

pale, weak, sickly; ineffective

She was so ill that she could muster only a ***wan*** *smile in response to his jokes, which usually had her doubled over with laughter.*

Synonyms: faint, feeble, pallid

• •

cautious, watchful, on guard

He was ***wary*** *of the suddenly kind attention from the classmates who usually made fun of him.*

Synonyms: attentive, vigilant

• •

full of whims, characterized by sudden and eccentric ideas

She wrote ***whimsical*** *tales about fairies and elves for children.*

Synonyms: fanciful, playful, wayward

WIELD
(weeld)

WILY
(WAHY-lee)

WRY
(rahy)

to use effectively; to exercise (power, influence, etc.)

*Having a deep respect for the teachers and great affection for the students at the school, she **wields** her authority as principal with grace.*

Synonyms: brandish, manage, manipulate; command, exercise

• •

full of tricks and stratagems that are intended to deceive or trap

*The **wily** student fooled his teachers through flattery, faked illnesses, and copied homework.*

Synonyms: crafty, cunning

• •

bent, twisted, or crooked; cleverly and ironically humorous

*Her **wry** jokes were a means of coping; they helped her make light of a bad situation.*

Synonyms: uneven; ironic

XENOPHOBIA

(zen-uh-FOH-bee-uh or zee-nuh-FOH-bee-uh)

YIELD

(yeeld)

ZENITH

(ZEE-nith)

fear or hatred of foreigners or of anything strange or foreign

After living for a few years with his daughter in Queens, where dozens upon dozens of different languages are spoken, the old man finally got over his lifelong ***xenophobia****.*

• •

(*v.*) to give up, surrender; to bring forth

Justly or not, we ***yielded*** *to their demands once they threatened us with a lawsuit.*

Synonyms: capitulate, relinquish, relent, submit; produce

(*n.*) that which is given or produced

Because there was so little rain this spring and summer, we are expecting a low crop ***yield*** *this year.*

Synonyms: output, earnings, harvest

• •

the highest point

Her record-breaking win of the Boston Marathon was the ***zenith*** *of her career as a runner.*

Synonyms: acme, culmination, summit

Part II

ABSOLUTE ZERO
(AB-suh-loot ZEE-roh)

ADAPTATION
(ad-up-TEY-shuhn)

AEROBIC ORGANISM
(uh-ROH-bik AWR-guh-niz-uhm)

–273.15°C, the temperature characterized by the cessation of molecular activity and the absence of heat

***Absolute zero** is only a theoretical possibility; even in the farthest reaches of outer space, heat left over from the Big Bang keeps the temperature from going any lower than about –235°C.*

• •

a change or changes in an organism or parts of an organism that make it more fit for survival in its environment

*Such traits as the long necks of giraffes are the results of **adaptations** to the environment.*

• •

an organism that uses oxygen in its metabolic processes

*Current thinking is that the first **aerobic organisms** on Earth evolved about 1.4 billion years ago, when sufficient oxygen for their survival had been released into the atmosphere.*

AMINO ACID
(uh-MEE-noh AS-id)

ANAEROBIC ORGANISM
(an-uh-ROH-bik AWR-guh-niz-uhm)

ATMOSPHERE
(AT-muhs-feer)

an organic acid containing at least one amino group, NH_2, and comprising the basic units of a protein

*Only twenty **amino acids** serve as the building blocks for an astonishing variety of proteins.*

• •

an organism that lives in the absence of free oxygen

*Earth's atmosphere once lacked free oxygen, and so the first life forms must have been **anaerobic**.*

• •

the mass of air that surrounds Earth; a gaseous envelope that encloses any celestial body

*The dense and cloudy **atmosphere** of Venus renders the surface of the planet so hot that lead could melt there.*

A

ATOM
(AT-uhm)

AUTOTROPH
(AW-tuh-trohf)

ACT SCIENCE

the smallest unit of an element having the chemical properties of the element and composed of electrons bound to a nucleus comprised of neutrons and protons

Having just one proton, one electron and no neutrons, the hydrogen atom is the lightest of all ***atoms****.*

• •

an organism that makes its own food, requiring only carbon in the form of carbon dioxide and inorganic nitrogen for its metabolic processes

Autotrophs *include green plants, algae, and some bacteria, and they are the producers in any given ecosystem.*

• •

BIG BANG
(big bang)

BIOME
(BAHY-ohm)

BOND
(bond)

ACT SCIENCE

the theoretical origin of the universe by which the universe itself was created in a sudden expansion from a single point of almost infinite density

*It is estimated that the **Big Bang** occurred some 13.8 billion years ago.*

• •

a distinct type of ecological community, such as grassland or tropical rain forest

*The **biomes** found in the continental United States include the temperate deciduous forest of the East, the grasslands of the Midwest, and the desert of the Southwest.*

• •

the attraction that holds atoms together in a molecule or crystal

*The compound sodium chloride is formed by an ionic **bond** between an atom of sodium and an atom of chlorine, whereas the compound hydrogen chloride is formed by a covalent bond between an atom of hydrogen and chlorine.*

CARBON CYCLE
(KAHR-buhn SAHY-kuhl)

CHROMOSOME
(KROH-muh-sohm)

CLIMATE
(KLAHY-mit)

ACT SCIENCE

the cycle by which carbon dioxide is fixed by photosynthesis and later released through respiration, decay, or combustion

Carbon forms part of all organic compounds, and so the ***carbon cycle*** *that circulates this element through the environment is necessary for life on Earth.*

the cycle by which carbon dioxide is fixed by photosynthesis

a structure contained within the nucleus of a eukaryote, containing the genetic material of the organism

Down syndrome is a disorder caused by the presence of an extra ***chromosome****.*

a set of conditions of temperature, precipitation, and wind typical for a specific region of Earth

The ***climate*** *in the valleys west of the Cascades of the Pacific Northwest is characterized by mild temperatures and abundant precipitation.*

COMPOUND
(KOM-pound)

CONDUCTION
(kuhn-DUK-shuhn)

CONVECTION
(kuhn-VEK-shuhn)

a pure substance composed of two or more elements

*The great variety of substances on Earth—and indeed, throughout the universe—is possible because atoms—such as atoms of the elements hydrogen and oxygen—combine to form **compounds**—such as H_2O, or water.*

• •

the transfer of heat between two parts of a system each having different temperatures

*Heat **conduction** occurs when rapidly moving particles transfer some of their energy to neighboring particles simply by interacting with them.*

• •

the transfer of heat by the circulation of a heated gas or liquid

***Convection** caused by radioactive decay in the mantle of Earth is believed to be the cause of plate movement, which in turn can cause earthquakes.*

CORE
(kour)

CRUST
(kruhst)

CURRENT
(KUHR-uhnt)

the central part of Earth, or, more broadly, the central part of a planet, moon, or star

*The molten **core** of Earth is about the same size as Mars.*

• •

the outer layer of Earth, or, more broadly, the outer layer of a planet or moon

*Earth's **crust** is 22 miles deep under the continents and 6 miles deep under the oceans.*

• •

the continuous flow of a gas or liquid in a particular direction

*The surface **currents** of the northern Indian Ocean change direction with the seasonal monsoon.*

DATA
(DEY-tuh or DAT-uh)

DIFFUSION
(dih-FYOO-zhuhn)

DNA
(dee-en-EY)

ACT SCIENCE

factual information, such as measurements or statistics

*As displayed on these graphs, the **data** clearly support your hypothesis.*

• •

the intermingling of molecules or ions by random thermal agitation

*To demonstrate **diffusion**, our teacher sprayed some perfume in one corner of the classroom, and its scent soon permeated the entire room.*

• •

acronym for deoxyribonucleic acid, a nucleic acid that is the molecular basis of heredity

*One goal of the Human Genome Project was to identify all of the genes encoded in human **DNA**.*

ECOSYSTEM
(EEK-oh-sis-tuhm)

ELECTROMAGNETISM
(ih-lek-troh-MAG-ni-ti-zuhm)

ELECTRON
(ih-LEK-tron)

E

a community of organisms and their environment

The extinction of just a few species can irrevocably alter or even destroy the ***ecosystem*** *in which the species took part.*

• •

a fundamental physical force having to do with charged particles and the emission and absorption of protons; phenomena associated with electric fields, magnetic fields, and their interactions

In the nineteenth century, James Clerk Maxwell showed that electric and magnetic fields travel together in waves, and his work with ***electromagnetism*** *set the stage for the greatest discoveries in twentieth-century physics.*

• •

a negatively charged particle

The configuration of ***electrons*** *in an atom determines its chemical nature.*

ELEMENT
(EL-uh-muhnt)

ENERGY
(EN-er-jee)

ENZYME
(EN-zahym)

one of the fundamental substances that cannot be broken down into simpler substances by means of chemistry

*Of the 118 known **elements**, about 20% have been created in a laboratory but do not exist in nature.*

• •

the capacity for doing work

*Kinetic **energy** has to do with motion; it is the energy of a body by virtue of the motion of the body or of a system by virtue of the motion of the particles in the system.*

• •

one of a group of proteins that stimulate particular biochemical reactions

***Enzymes** regulate all sorts of chemical reactions within organisms, such as the digestion of food.*

EQUILIBRIUM
(ee-kwuh-LI-bree-uhm)

EUKARYOTE
(yoo-KAR-ee-oht)

EVOLUTION
(ev-uh-LOO-shuhn)

a state of balance between opposing forces; a condition in which a reversible chemical reaction proceeds in both directions at equal rates

Homeostasis is a form of dynamic ***equilibrium*** *by which a biological system maintains its stability in response to changing conditions.*

• •

an organism composed of one or more cells having a nucleus and distinct organelles

Eukaryotes *are thought to have evolved through the symbiotic merging of different types of bacteria.*

• •

the development of a species over history, or the process of genetic modifications by which such development occurs

Although the species Homo sapiens *evolved some 100,000 or 200,000 years ago, human* ***evolution*** *can be said to have begun millions of years before that, in the Miocene Epoch.*

FOSSIL
(FOS-uhl)

FUSION
(FYOO-zhuhn)

F

the remnant, impression, or trace of an organism from a former geologic age

*Very few organisms remain as **fossils**, for only hard parts such as shells or bone are readily preserved.*

• •

a nuclear reaction in which the nuclei of atoms are combined to form the nuclei of heavier atoms

*The heat of the sun is produced by the **fusion** of hydrogen atoms to create helium.*

• •

GALAXY
(GAL-uhk-see)

GAS
(gas)

GENE
(jeen)

a system of stars held together by gravity

*Located about 2,480,000 light-years from Earth, the Andromeda Galaxy is the spiral **galaxy** nearest to the Milky Way.*

• •

a fluid having neither shape nor volume and tending to expand indefinitely

*Water vapor is a **gas** that condenses to form precipitation.*

• •

a specific sequence of nucleotides in DNA or RNA that encodes the structure of a protein and is associated with the expression of a trait in an organism

*Traits such as left-handedness may be linked to a single **gene**.*

GENOTYPE
(JEE-noh-tahyp)

GLUCOSE
(GLOO-kohs)

GRAVITY
(GRAV-i-tee)

the genetic composition of an organism or group of organisms, in whole or in part

*Identical twins share the same **genotype**.*

---

a simple sugar that is widely found in nature

***Glucose** is the source of energy for cells.*

---

a fundamental physical force having to do with the attraction between two masses; the force by which bodies tend to fall toward the center of a celestial body, such as Earth

*In his general theory of relativity, Einstein showed that **gravity** is the result of a curvature in space-time.*

HABITAT
(HAB-i-tat)

HALF-LIFE
(HAF-lahyf)

HEREDITY
(huh-RED-i-tee)

the environment in which an organism naturally lives

*Because of our ability to create tools and culture, humans have been able to adapt to just about every **habitat** on Earth.*

• •

the time in which half of the atoms of a radioactive substance disintegrates

*Carbon-14 has a **half-life** of about 5,730 years, and measuring its presence in organic remains can be used to estimate the age of the remains.*

• •

the sum of the genetic traits received from one's ancestors; the genetic transmission of such traits

*In the 1950s, the investigations of Francis Crick and James Watson into the structure of DNA revealed the mechanism's underlying **heredity**.*

H

HETEROTROPH
(HET-er-uh-trof)

HYPOTHESIS
(hahy-POTH-uh-sis)

an organism that requires organic compounds of carbon and nitrogen for its metabolic processes

***Heterotrophs** include all animals and fungi, and they are the consumers in any given ecosystem.*

a proposition or propositions given in explanation of some phenomena and set forth in order to be tested through experiment

*The experiment showed that her original **hypothesis** was incorrect, but revealed a more compelling explanation.*

IMMUNITY
(ih-MYOO-ni-tee)

INERTIA
(in-UR-shuh)

ION
(AHY-on)

the ability to resist a particular disease

*My **immunity** from chicken pox comes from having had the disease as a child; others obtain their immunity from the disease by having a vaccination.*

• •

the property by which matter remains at rest or in uniform motion along a straight line unless acted upon by a force

*If a car comes to a sudden stop, the passengers in the car continue to move forward because of **inertia**.*

• •

a positively or negatively charged atom or group of atoms, having lost or gained one or more electrons; a cation is positively charged and an anion is negatively charged

*Sodium chloride is formed through the bonding of a sodium **ion** and a chlorine ion.*

I

ISOTONIC
(ahy-suh-TON-ik)

ISOTOPE
(AHY-suh-tohp)

ACT SCIENCE

(also, *isosmotic*) related to solutions having equal osmotic pressure

*An **isotonic** saline solution has the same concentration of salt as the blood.*

any of two or more forms of a chemical element having the same atomic number, or number of protons, but a different atomic mass, or different number of neutrons

*The element fluorine has only one stable **isotope**, fluorine-19, whereas xenon has nine.*

KREBS CYCLE
(KREBZ SAHY-kuhl)

the final series of reactions in aerobic metabolism, which uses oxygen, produces carbon dioxide, and forms ATP

*The **Krebs cycle** is part of the process by which cells obtain energy from organic material.*

LIGHT-YEAR

(LAHYT-yeer)

ACT SCIENCE

5.88 trillion miles, an astronomical unit of measure equal to the distance light travels in one year

Alpha Centauri is composed of three stars, one of which, Proxima Centauri, is 4.2 ***light-years*** *away and the closest star to our Sun.*

• •

ACT SCIENCE

MANTLE
(MAN-tl)

MASS
(mas)

MATTER
(MA-tuhr)

ACT SCIENCE

the part of Earth below the crust and outside of the core

*Although the **mantle** is solid, it is not static.*

• •

the measure of matter contained in a body

*Though you would weigh less on Mars than you do on Earth, your **mass** would remain the same.*

• •

a substance that takes up space, has mass, and is composed of atoms

*Einstein's famous equation, $E = mc^2$, essentially states that **matter** and energy can be converted into each other.*

M

METABOLISM
(muh-TAB-uh-li-zuhm)

MINERAL
(MIN-ruhl or MIN-er-uhl)

MITOSIS
(mahy-TOH-sis)

ACT SCIENCE

M

the physical and chemical processes by which energy is made available for the organism

*Because of her speedy **metabolism**, she could eat just about as much as she wanted and more without gaining any weight.*

• •

a solid homogenous substance with a crystalline structure that occurs in nature

*Rocks are composed of one or more **minerals**; limestone, for example, is primarily composed of the mineral calcite, whereas granite is composed of quartz, feldspar, mica, and amphibole.*

• •

the process by which the nucleus of a dividing cell itself divides into two nuclei, each with the same number of chromosomes as the original nucleus

*After **mitosis**, the two resulting daughter cells are genetically identical.*

M

MOLE
(mohl)

MOLECULE
(MOL-uh-kyool)

MOMENTUM
(moh-MEN-tuhm)

the molecular weight of a substance, in grams

*One **mole** of oxygen has the same number of atoms as a mole of carbon-12 but a greater mass.*

• •

the smallest unit of a substance having the properties of that substance and composed of one or more atoms

*One **molecule** of water (H_2O), consists of two atoms of hydrogen (H) and one atom of oxygen (O).*

• •

a property of a moving body, equal to the product of the mass of the body and its velocity

***Momentum** refers not just to the motion of a body, but to the power of a moving body.*

MUTATION
(myoo-TEY-shuhn)

• •

MUTUALISM
(MYOO-choo-wuh-li-zuhm)

• •

M

a change in hereditary material resulting from a change in a gene or chromosome; an individual organism or species resulting from such a change

*A silent **mutation** is a change in the DNA sequence that results in no observable change in the traits of an organism.*

• •

a symbiotic relationship that is mutually beneficial to each organism involved

*The relationship between bees and flowers is an example of **mutualism**.*

• •

NEUTRON
(NOO-tron)

NITROGEN CYCLE
(NAHY-truh-juhn SAHY-kuhl)

NUCLEAR REACTION
(NOO-klee-uhr ree-AK-shuhn)

N

a particle without charge and with mass slightly greater than that of a proton that forms part of the nuclei of all atoms but hydrogen

Each of the three isotopes of carbon has the same number of protons but a different number of ***neutrons****: carbon-12 has six neutrons, carbon-13 has seven neutrons, and carbon-14, a radioactive isotope, has eight neutrons.*

• •

the cycle of natural processes by which nitrogen passes from air to soil to organisms and then returns to air or soil, and so on

One stage of the ***nitrogen cycle*** *is nitrogen fixation, by which free nitrogen is combined with other elements to form such compounds as ammonia, nitrates, and nitrites.*

• •

a change in an atomic nucleus, caused by bombarding it with an energetic particle and resulting in the emission of a nucleon, alpha particle, or other particle

In the ***nuclear reaction*** *known as fission, the nucleus of a heavy element is split into two and emits free neutrons.*

NUCLEOTIDE

(NOO-klee-uh-tahyd)

• •

NUCLEUS

(NOO-klee-uhs)

• •

N

one of a group of molecules that, when linked together, form the basic units of DNA and RNA; a nucleotide is composed of a ribose or deoxyribose sugar, a phosphate group, and adenine, cytosine, guanine, thymine (in DNA), or uracil (in RNA)

*The order of **nucleotides** in a gene determines the order of amino acids in a protein.*

• •

(in biology) an organelle that is enclosed within a membrane and involved in such essential cellular processes as reproduction and protein synthesis

*A mature human red blood cell has no **nucleus**.*

(in physical science) the positively charged part of an atom, composed of protons and neutrons

*The **nucleus** of a hydrogen atom has just one proton and no neutrons.*

• •

ORBITAL
(AWR-bi-tl)

ORGANISM
(AWR-guh-niz-uhm)

OSMOSIS
(oz-MOH-sis)

ACT SCIENCE

a region around the nucleus of an atom that may contain one, two, or no electrons

Valence electrons are those in the outermost ***orbital*** *of an atom and are involved in the formation of chemical bonds.*

• •

an individual living being

An ***organism*** *can be comprised of a single cell or of millions upon millions of specialized, interdependent cells.*

• •

the movement of a solvent through a semipermeable membrane into a solution in which the concentration of solute is higher, which tends to equalize the concentration of solute on either side of the membrane

Water enters the roots of plants primarily by ***osmosis****.*

PH
(pee-EYCH)

PHENOTYPE
(FEE-nuh-tahyp)

PHEROMONE
(FER-uh-mohn)

the measure of acidity or alkalinity of a solution on a scale in which acidity is represented by values less than 7, alkalinity by values greater than 7, and neutrality by 7

Lemon juice is acidic, with a ***pH*** *somewhere between 2 and 3.*

• •

the observable characteristics of an organism, resulting from the interaction of its genotype and environment

Genes for a large, robust organism may not be expressed in the ***phenotype*** *of that individual if, for example, the food supply were inadequate.*

• •

a chemical substance produced and released by an animal that influences the behavior or physiology of others in the same species

The activities of ant colonies are coordinated through messages transmitted by ***pheromones****.*

PHOTON
(FOH-ton)

PLATE
(pleyt)

PROTEIN
(PROH-teen)

a particle or quantum of electromagnetic radiation

*The term **photon** derives from the Greek word meaning* from light, *and the particle itself travels at the speed of light.*

• •

any of the large, moveable units of Earth's lithosphere, or crust and upper mantle

***Plate** tectonics has to do with the movements of Earth's plates and explains such cataclysmic events as earthquakes as well as such long-term changes as continental drift.*

• •

one of a group of complex compounds that are composed of amino acids joined by peptide bonds and that constitute a great portion of the mass of any organism

***Proteins** serve such essential functions in organisms as catalyzing chemical reactions, serving as structural elements of cells, and, as antibodies, protecting animals from disease.*

P

PROTON

(PROH-ton)

a positively charged particle that forms part of the nuclei of all atoms

The atomic number of an element corresponds to the number of ***protons*** *in its nucleus.*

RADIATION
(rey-dee-EY-shuhn)

RADIOACTIVITY
(rey-dee-oh-ak-TIV-i-tee)

REACTION
(ree-AK-shuhn)

the emission of energy as particles or waves

*Solar **radiation** is the primary source of energy on Earth.*

• •

the disintegration of the nuclei of atoms of some elements through the emission of radiation

***Radioactivity** can damage the cells in your body.*

• •

a chemical change resulting from the interaction of chemical agents, or the process of such a chemical change

*Fire is the result of a chemical **reaction** between oxygen and a fuel.*

R

REGENERATION
(ri-jen-uh-REY-shuhn)

RESPIRATION
(res-puh-REY-shuhn)

RNA
(ahr-en-EY)

ACT SCIENCE

the replacement of a body part through the growth of new tissue

Some starfish can replace lost arms through ***regeneration****.*

• •

the processes by which an organism is supplied with oxygen and relieved of carbon dioxide

Larger animals use structures such as tracheae, gills, and lungs for ***respiration****.*

• •

acronym for ribonucleic acid, a nucleic acid that is associated with chemical activities within cells

RNA *is the carrier of genetic material in some viruses.*

R

ROTATION
(roh-TEY-shuhn)

ACT SCIENCE

the movement of Earth or another celestial body around a central axis

The apparent rising and setting of the Sun is caused not by the movement of the Sun itself, but by the ***rotation*** *of Earth on its axis.*

• •

SOLUTION

(suh-LOO-shuhn)

SPECIES

(SPEE-sheez or SPEE-seez)

SPORE

(spour)

ACT SCIENCE

S

the process by which a gas, liquid, or solid solute is homogenously mixed into a gas, liquid, or solid solvent, or the mixture created by such a process

*We made a simple **solution** by dissolving salt in water.*

• •

a group of related organisms capable of interbreeding

*The fossil record reveals that there have been many **species** of humans, but only one,* Homo sapiens, *has survived to our time.*

• •

a reproductive body capable of developing into a new individual organism either directly or after fusing with another spore

*Fungi such as mushrooms reproduce by generating **spores** that grow into new individuals.*

S

SYMBIOSIS

(sim-bee-OH-sis or *sim-bahy-OH-sis)*

ACT SCIENCE

S

the living together of two unlike organisms

Symbiosis *includes such beneficial relationships as those between cows and the bacteria in their guts, as well as parasitic relationships, which can harm the host.*

• •

THEORY
(THEE-uh-ree or *THEER-ee)*

TRAIT
(treyt)

TRANSCRIPTION
(tran-SKRIP-shuhn)

ACT SCIENCE

a set of scientifically tested and accepted principles given in explanation of some phenomena

*Einstein's **theory** of relativity transformed our understanding of both space and time.*

an inherited characteristic

*Such **traits** as eye color, hair color, and height are only some of the more obvious characteristics one inherits from his or her parents.*

the process of creating a molecule of messenger RNA from the information encoded in DNA

*The strand of RNA that results from the process of **transcription** is complementary to but not a copy of the strand of DNA on which it is based.*

TRANSLATION
(tranz-LEY-shuhn)

TRANSLOCATION
(tranz-loh-KEY-shuhn)

TURGOR
(TUR-ger)

the process of creating a molecule of protein from the information encoded in messenger RNA

*A codon is comprised of a specific sequence of three nucleotides, which in **translation** corresponds with a specific amino acid.*

the movement of part of a chromosome to a different chromosome

*Chromosomal **translocation** is associated with certain cancers, such as leukemia.*

the normal distention or rigidity of plant cells caused by the pressure within the cells

*If you do not water your plants, the **turgor** pressure in their cells will decrease, and the plants will begin to wilt.*

UNIVERSE
(YOO-ni-vuhrs)

VELOCITY
(vuh-LOS-i-tee)

the entire body of matter and phenomena

*Evidence shows that all galaxies are receding from each other, which means that the **universe** continues to expand even 13.8 billion years after the Big Bang.*

• •

the rate of change in the position of a body moving along a straight line

*Escape **velocity** is the minimum speed required for one body to escape the gravitational field of another.*

• •

WATER CYCLE
(WOT-er SAHY-kuhl)

WAVE
(weyv)

WORK
(wuhrk)

the cycle in which water evaporates into the atmosphere, returns to Earth as liquid or solid precipitation, and then evaporates again

Clouds, rain, and snow are some of the more apparent aspects of the ***water cycle****.*

• •

a disturbance that transfers energy from point to point in a medium or in space

Because light ***waves*** *travel so much faster than sound waves, you will see a distant flash of lightning before you hear the accompanying crack of thunder.*

• •

a transference of energy, the product of force and the distance through which the force acts

The displacement of a body from one place to another is considered ***work****, as is the compression of a gas or the rotation of a shaft.*